MY THERAPY JOURNAL:
A JOURNEY OF HEALING

MICAH MASON

Author's Tranquility Press
Marietta, Georgia

Micah Mason /Author's Tranquility Press
2706 Station Club Drive SW
Marietta, GA 30060
www.authorstranquilitypress.com

Ordering Information:
Quantity sales. Special discounts are available on quantity purchases by corporations, associations, and others. For details, contact the "Special Sales Department" at the address above.

My Therapy Journal: A Journey of Healing/ Micah Mason
Hardback: 978-1-958179-63-5
Paperback: 978-1-958179-04-8
eBook: 978-1-958179-05-5

Dedication

The quilt on the cover of the book was made by the nine-year-old victim of molestation. She worked on the quilt indoors to avoid the neighbor outside.

This book is dedicated to my poetry pals. Both gave me unconditional love and pointed out my strengths. And to all the children who were molested or raped and didn't get to voice their pain, anger, and depression. I hope these poems give you a voice.

And thanks to my friend for his technical support to fill in my gaps of knowledge about the computer.

INTRODUCTION

As I awakened from years of repression, depression, and denial, I decided I needed counseling for the years of molestation I had suffered as a child. It started with a seven-year-old Brownie going to a neighbor's house to get an order for Girl Scout calendars. It seemed like an over-done, slobbery kiss as I left, but at seven you're really not sure. That was the beginning of four years of hiding or being caught and molested. This evading and avoiding contact led to much stress and a state of chronic hypervigilance from age seven to eleven. As I discussed these things with my counselor, he suggested, as "homework" that I should start journaling. The journaling began as prose-like diary entries but quickly changed to poetry after starting an American literature class.

These poems are raw, rough, and straight from my mind, heart, and soul. Though not elegant in the normal literary sense, they are elegant in their truthful expression of unfiltered emotions. They express the tender, painful wounds of depression to the point of feeling the tears rolling down my cheeks. Some can take wings of flight from pure joy finding healing in the evolution of the journey that is life. We always have the freedom of choice in how we respond to life events and our feelings. We can allow the tears of depression to drown us or they can become the saline that cleanses our wounds. When withholding, tears can grow to the steam of anger that leads to hurting others because we are in pain. Tears of sadness can weaken our resolves, so we give up hope and drown ourselves in alcohol or drugs. I chose to eat too much.

In the beginning, my choices were driven by depression which was not wise due to the binding despair and low self-esteem. But as I moved along the trails of life and different styles of therapy, so enough healing took place, I made better choices toward new steps. I moved from talk therapy to behavior modification and finally eye movement desensitization and reprocessing (EMDR).

These are the poems of my therapy journal that I started in the mid-eighties' and have continued to the present day. As you watch the evolution of my healing of my moods, so do my poems evolve. Note also the change from self-absorbed pain to sassy looks at my broadened world.

By the grace of God, we will all evolve into another being through the pathway of life. Sometimes events are emotionally filled with pain, sadness, and fear, but love, hope, and faith can keep us glued together enough to bring us face to face with our purpose. When we can see that purpose, we can put energy into our lives to move toward goals. Then the journey moves from mere existence to life evolved, an evolution of body, spirit, and mind. Through this evolution, we transform from a cocooned insect frightened of being squashed, into a butterfly that can go to any height you can dream, imagine, or create. As I found my life purpose of healing and teaching others as a nurse, my journal can now be one of my tools of healing for others. So I am sharing my journal of life and healing in the hope it helps someone else to find healing. These poems show a wide range of emotions and experiences as I opened doors to my life and moved forward to new horizons. I also share insights on the life-happenings that gave birth to these poems. If you find something in them that I did not see as I wrote them and it does you good, take it. If bad, then let it go.

Contents

TOUCH 1

PAIN MAKES ME KNOW I'M ALIVE 2

HOW BARREN 3

TO MY SONS! 4

BART'S A BRAT, ... 6

I WONDER 7

AHHH! 8

EMOTIONAL PATHS 9

HOPE FOR JOY 10

THE GREATEST LESSON 11

A MILLION TEARS 12

SELF- INFLICTED ISOLATION 13

THE ONE WHO SHARED THE SECRET Oh! Angelica, my
dear Angelica! 15

MY PRESENT GUILT 16

TO TRAVIS MY LOVE 17

SUBCONSCIOUS EXPRESSIONS 18

TO EZRA 19

IN CONTRADICTION TO HIS LOVE 20

UNFINISHED BUSINESS 21

BARED BY THE TALES 22

MY SISTER'S TRUE DEPTH 23

SICKNESS ON SICKNESS 24

DADDY SAYS 25

ON THAT LANE 26

MY POOR MOTHER'S FRUSTRATION 27

THROUGH A MILLION TEARS 28

A MILLION TO ONE 29

PRAISE TO THE FATHER 31

WITH THE DEVIL INSIDE 32

GOD SEEING ALL 33

REMEMBER WHEN 34

LOVE YOU 35

A SANDCASTLE BE 36

TO DONNA 37

LOVE AND DESIRE 38

GRANDMA DEAR 39

A PARADOX 40

DARKNESS 41

IN THE STILL OF THE NIGHT 42

LOVE TRAVIS 43

CLEANSED 45

A TOUCH OF LIFE AND HEALTH 46

HE TOUCHED ME 47

OF FLYING SNAKES 48

CERTAIN NOISES, SMELLS, AND SIGHTS 49

AMNESIA 50

WET AGAIN 51

THE TUNNEL 52

SUNBEAMS 53

BABE AT BREAST 54

A SPECIAL MOMENT WITH A DOCTOR AND WIFE 55

TIME TO LEAVE 56

WHAT THE NURSES SAW 57

THE HAT 58

SHE'S GOT LEGS 59

LAWN CHAIRS 60

I HATE HOT DOGS 61

TOASTED MARSHMALLOWS..62

WITH HIS WIFE IN THE NEXT ROOM................................63

DIVING DEEP 64

I KNOW..66

I COULD BE..67

HE DOESN'T UNDERSTAND..68

I LIKE SCHOOL 69

GIVING UP IS HARD..70

I WANT GOD IN MY HEART...71

STAND UP FOR YOUR RIGHTS..72

CIGARS..73

SOMEONE KNEW 74

SHE KNEW TOO 75

HOW DID MY SISTER FEEL? 76

A FAMILY REUNION 77

MAKE EVERYDAY SPECIAL...79

GENETICS AND GOD'S GIFTS..80

GLASS TRAP 81

LIKE A TEENAGER 83

BORN OF SHAME...84

I HATE SNAKES 85

WHEN LOSING CONTROL...86

BROCK...87

SHAME, SHAME ON YOU..88

OF ROCKS AND ISLANDS...89

HATE 90

COUSIN TO COUSIN 91

NOT WORTHY 92

JANUARY 1986..93

WINTER WIND 94

TORN IN PIECES 96
ALICE OF THE LOOKING-GLASS 97
ALONE WITH LONELINESS 98
GHOSTS 100
! ! ! FREE ! ! !... 101
FOR BETSY 102
DESPAIR 103
EMOTIONAL DEATH 104
NIGHTMARE CAGE 106
TO JUSTIN 107
TRUST 108
HAPPINESS' HORIZON 109
TO MARGARET... 110
HERE'S TO YOU, DION ! 111
TRAPPED... 113
TORTURED LIFE... 115
TRIBUTE TO SELF-HELP BOOKS 116
VAMPIRE'S VICTIM.. 118
DIRECTIONS... 119
CINDER CITY 120
3 BULLETS IN THE FLOOR 122
DROUGHT OF "93" 123
I AM A PERSON.. 124
ANGER 125
I BELIEVE IN ME.. 126
GORE ORPHANAGE 127
SOME FUN LIMERICKS... 128
THE FLOWER MAN 128
COLOR COMES TO MY WORLD 131
BLUE CHRISTMAS WRAP... 132

LORD OF LIGHT 133

SHUT DOWN 135

RELENTLESS LOVE 136

THE BRIDE OF FRANKENSTEIN 137

SYMPHONY OF SYMPATHY 138

ASHLEY'S POEM 139

JOY'S SACRIFICE 140

HEADACHES WITHOUT END 141

MISSING TERRI 142

THE FORTRESS 143

LONGINGS 145

FOUND POEM from an OLD TEXTBOOK 146

HOPE FLOATS 147

OCHER STAIN 148

TO DROWN OR NOT TO DROWN? 149

HOPE 150

AWAY WITH SADNESS 151

NIGHT VIGIL FOR MOM 152

THE WEIGHT OF MY PEARLS 153

DAD 154

DAD's SONG OF LOW SELF-ESTEEM 155

TO DAD 156

CRAZY KARINA 157

THE PAST 158

THE LAND OF TRUMPMANIA 159

TEARS FOR MY MOTHER 161

TO BEATRICE 162

GOOD-BYE TO DONATA 163

CLIMBING OUT 165

A YEAR OF LOSSES 166

CONTROL ADDICT'S POWER 167

LIFE 168

GLORIA 169

WAIT AND SEE 170

GO ON FAITH 171

A PATH OF LEARNING 172

OUT OF FOCUS 173

TENDER MOMENT 174

PARADOX TRAP 175

HEALING SCARS 176

ARCTIC NIGHTSHIFT 177

KINDNESS 178

REVELATION IN THE NIGHT 179

DREAMERS 180

PURPOSE 181

SUICIDAL THOUGHT 182

IN YOUR THOUGHTS 183

GOD IS LOVE 184

DAYS OF SADNESS 185

THE TEAR 187

THE HIGH RISE 188

YOUTH RE-VISITED 189

FALLING WISDOM 190

LIVING WELL 191

ABUSE OF SILENCING 192

FOREVER GREEN 193

DAYS OF GRAY 194

STRENGTH TOGETHER 195

I NEED TO BE NEEDED 196

SUMMER DROUGHT 197

MY SONS 198
GIFT FROM MY SON 199
SPECIAL FRIENDS 200
Introduction to New Poems 201
RELATIONSHIP 203
HIDDEN BUNNIES 204
AM I? 205
SUPER HEROES 206
HAIKU 207
BROKEN 208
JOYFUL POTENTIAL 209
ZERO 210
FINDING JOY 211
INAPPROPRIATE 212
DOGGY BLUES 213
MY LOST MOM 214
MAKES MIGRAINES MEANINGFUL 215
SORRY TO MY SON 216
INVISIBLE 217
SECRECTS 218
MY EVERYWHERE THERAPIST 219
LYING LEADER 220
I NEED A GOOD CRY 221
BIPOLAR ME 222
PRODUCT PILES 223
EMPTY WITHOUT YOU 224
THE POWER OF POETRY 225
?WHY? 226
A CHICKEN'S COUNSEL 227
THE EMPTY ZONE 228

AFTERMATH OF AN ARGUMENT 229

47 ASPIRINS 230

TODAY AT A GLANCE.. 231

TRUMP – McCONNELL VANITY WALL........................ 232

CONDESCENSION 233

WRONG 234

BELOW THE DOME... 235

FILLING SPACE... 236

ENDLESS.. 237

WHY IS EXISTENCE? 238

NEVER.. 239

DISMISS 240

PURE EVIL... 241

BEAUTY ON THE BEACH... 242

BUTTERFLY GIRL 243

CORONAVIRUS... 244

DON'T FEED THE GREED 245

COVID-19 PANDEMIC 246

HIS SLAVE.. 247

DEARLY.. 248

A THANK YOU 249

STROKES.. 250

UNDERSTANDING THE NOW 251

BERNIE BROS 252

UNSTUPIFYING OF AMERICA.................................... 253

HIAKU.. 254

GROWN-UP ADULTS 254

APRIL TORNADO.. 255

HIAKU.. 256

GETTING UP... 257

AGAIN!..258

GROWING FEAR OF NUMBERS...........................259

CIRCLE OF NOISE...260

LOST SKILLS 261

SELFISH AND CRUEL 262

HOSTA..264

EMOTIONAL CONTROL 265

MISSING THE CALL...266

THE ARGUMENT 267

MAGNETIC REPULSION 268

LITTLE RED RIDING HOOD 269

PTSD – COVID-19...270

DAILY MOURNING...271

UNMASKED TRUTH 272

HIDDEN BEAUTY...273

NON – SYBIL..274

PERSONHOOD DISMISSED.................................275

"MASKED VOICES" 276

THE TEAR..277

THE PROTOCOL 278

ASEXUAL...279

NO! AUTO MOBILE..280

SABRINA'S SMILE..281

FOOD PHOBIC..282

COVID CRISIS...283

WHAT IS HAPPENING? 284

BEATEN DOWN by CHAOS 285

ANXIETY 286

The DON of DEATH'S DOMAIN...........................287

LOVE ME AS I AM..288

SELFISH SHORTSIGHTEDNESS 290

PEDOPHILE'S PARADISE 291

STATIC STATE of ANXIETY 292

INTRODUCTION TO POEMS FROM MICAH MASON'S
FACEBOOK 294

PEDOPHILE'S PARADISE 295

TEMPORARILY CLEAN 296

TRUST FACTORS 297

FORGIVENESS FOR ME 299

MOURNING MY LIFE 300

THE HEALING GOES ON 301

RINGING MEMORY 302

INSURRECTION 304

PATIENCE ZONE 306

WEIGHING IN ON ISSUES 307

PATHETIC PUNK PRESIDENT 308

THE BRIDGE OF OBSTRUCTION 309

CAR POOL FOG 311

COUP BY CULT 313

FOOD FEAR 315

SAFE CHOICE? 316

WISHING 317

PARASITIC 318

REFUSED TO RECEIVE 319

BOOGERS BE GONE 320

DRAGON-EYE MOON 321

TOO MUCH ICK 322

ON THE MENU 323

THE SOLUTION MENU 325

PASSIVE SUICIDE 326

FLY FROM STRESS 328

SHARED STRESS 329

THE ESCAPE DOOR 330

SOUR MILK 331

STANDING TALL 332

MID-APRIL SNOW 333

CLIMATE CHANGE IS REAL! 334

MORAL LEPER...................................335

WHAT I SEE...................................336

HOLLOW VESSEL...................................337

VAX TO RELAX 338

ORIANA...................................339

ABSENT HERO...................................340

HIS SMELL...................................342

THE WRITER'S AWARD...................................343

VERONICA'S HOME...................................344

THE RAIN OF LIES...................................345

MY TWIN, MY HERO...................................347

HIS WINNER'S TROPHY...................................348

ENERGY STEALING CLIMATE...................................349

WHATEVER IT TAKES...................................350

NO SEWING MACHINE NOW 351

A DOOR TO CONTROL 352

HATE OF LIFE 354

AMERICA SINKS 355

TROPHY OF CONTROL...................................356

THE PRICE OF LIFE...................................357

NO COMPUTER BRAIN 358

NO SOCIAL RELATIONSHIP...................................359

MY REPEATING HISTORY...................................361

MY HOARDER'S HOUSE.. 363

LACK IN ABUNDANCE 364

THE CAT LADY'S RATIO 366

THE VIEW BEFORE YOU 367

DEVOID SOULS.. 368

SAGED INSIGHT... 369

USED UP.. 370

EPILOGUE: 371

HYMN RESOURCE LIST:... 372

    SELF-HELP BOOKS LIST and INTERNET WEBSITE LIST

.... 379

TOUCH

Touch or be touched.
What an empty,
Inescapable prison
Is this black hole
That I call existence.
How frighteningly lonely.
Eternal void,
Self-encapsulated
Into a vacuum.

(To be safe you can self-imprison in an emotion-free
bubble.)

PAIN MAKES ME KNOW I'M ALIVE

I have to wonder whether
I actually exist.
Were it not for the pain,
I would say no, I do not exist.
Only the pain keeps me wondering
And hedging at a yes.
Could it be I fear the loss of pain,
Whether as guilt or physical aches,
Because then I would cease to exist?
Only living things feel pain.
I have pain, I am alive.

(Chronic depression, hypervigilance, and chronic stress
all cause bodily pain from inflammation.)

HOW BARREN

Oh! How barren desolate is her heart
In a feelingless existence thou art.
No pangs of love or pangs of hate.
Nothing more pierces her armor plate.
Chaste, impotent, barren always be;
Cold, lonely, and ever empty is she.
Oh! How barren is the house
That lays without people or mouse.
Or their happy ringing noise
Enveloped in drifts of snow.
Chaste, impotent, barren always;
Cold, lonely, and ever empty is she.

(So much of your world doesn't feel emotionally safe, so
you isolate more and more -- consciously or
unconsciously. Walls go up, and you are more and more
alone. When both parties in a relationship are damaged
from childhood events, wall obstruct any possibility of a
relationship. A state of clinical loneliness becomes status
quo.)

TO MY SONS!

I know that now
You are not old enough
To understand.
But when
You are older and can,
Then I hope
You will read this.
You stomp about some days
Having fit upon fit
Because you can't have your way.
You yell,
"I don't love you Mommy
Not anymore",
And stomp, fuss and cry.
But think of this son:
We can't all have our own way
All of the time
Without infringing, using, and abusing others.
There are many times when
I'd love my own way,
But you don't see me
Stomping and crying.
Although, sometimes I fuss.
Hey you!
"When was this time
You wanted your way and
Gave in to me instead?"
Take for example,

Sometime when I was sick
And wanted nothing more
Than to be alone in my bed.
My responsibility was
First for your care,
So on the couch I stayed
Listening to you bicker and
Fight with your brother.
Meanwhile, I felt more tired
And my head split
Wider with pain.
But I did it without
Stomping, fussing, crying or
Demanding my way.
Love, your mother.

(I learned in time when I was down in the dumps the
kids acted out more and we fell into downward spirals,
feeding negatively off of each other's dark moods.)

BART'S A BRAT,

And I'm going mad
Cry, cry, cry or
Giggle, trouble, giggle.

(Another downward spiral with Mr. Hyperactive ADD
man.)

I WONDER

I wonder about why I feel so trapped?
Sliding into thoughts of
What unbalances older people the most,
Then I say, "Ah! lack of control!"
And where does this exist in my life,
So young and vital?
"Everywhere!" comes the answer,
With the children,
I lack the control to make them behave
As they must toward each other
So I can get even the
Most minimal task done.
With my job,
I lack the control to feel secure
And feel I will not lose my job.
Then they make a change,
So I don't know what my job is.
With my husband,
I lack the control to make him
Complete anything:
Assorted projects with house, vehicles,
Gardens or animals --
To follow through with responsibilities,
To take part in caring for the children,
To have conversations that are actual
Communication.
People and actions need completion for
Stabilization.

(Incomplete tasks leave emotional imbalances, that lead
to a lot of emotional egg-shell walking. This is not
healthy.)

AHHH!

"Hello, Dear!
What was the name of the water hauler?"
"Why do you need it?", says he
"There are clothes in my washer,
Two inches of water,
Half a cup of soap,
Dirty diapers,
No water in the cistern,
Six acres of dishes in the sink,
A pie to bake --
Shall I go on?"
"You'll what?"
"I need water now!"

(My husband was a control addict from his out-of-control childhood. Controlling money and spending was a chronic problem. We -- the kids and myself -- suffered because he won't buy into public water sources.)

EMOTIONAL PATHS

I found my life filled
With an emotional pain
I could not describe,
And God led me into nursing.
I felt life was a form of hell
Not understanding why I must live.
God led me to work with cancer patients,
I saw how strongly they clung to life.
I wondered why I should keep trying
When life was so painful.
Then God showed me that the heart
Could be mended and renewed
On the cardiac floor.

(When my patients clung desperately to life, I started
examining why I rejected life. What was wrong with me,
my life, and my views.)

HOPE FOR JOY

Children running in free circles,
Like leaves swirling and
Dancing in the breeze.
Such uninhibited freedom;
Such a thrill to be alive.
Let me feel it in
My heart and soul.
Let the very core of me,
Fill me with the joys of life.

(This showed hope that I would seek joy and want to seek joy. That part of me was not dead just repressed.)

THE GREATEST LESSON

We humans are not orphans
The kind and gracious God
Has fostered and adopted,
But the very children of God
Who are loved unconditionally,
And blessed with the
Inheritance of eternal life.
As so-called orphans
Searching for love,
God is there, a natural parent.
Jesus was not the only child
He is just the first to
Recognize his relationship.

(I felt alienated emotionally from my parents -- like they never bonded with me. It was good to see the true and deep relational bond we have with God. The whole Bible is about showing us how to maintain our relationship with Him.)

A MILLION TEARS

A million tears
To ease my fears;
Will not these walls erode,
Protector of the secret untold.
Touched by my Father --
Why would He bother?
To touch this leper,
Through loving endeavor,
His caring to impart,
Infiltrating my heart.

(Because of childhood events and ongoing experiences, I erected walls to protect myself from further abuse, and I felt contaminated. I could not figure out why God would risk touching me, even to heal me, but His presence was constant.)

SELF- INFLICTED ISOLATION

To feel so unworthy, unclean,
As to never be touched.
No warmth of caring to glean,
Loveless my heart clutched.

God so near I can see Him,
Yet I won't open up.
I hide myself on a whim,
Again He asks me to sup.

But I away did turn
Hiding myself again.
His power I fear would burn,
So more I lose not gain.

"Why do you fear Me?"
He asked most sincerely,
"Your life with mine should be
I care for you most dearly."

"Allow me to touch you
I want to most truly"
I want you, very much too."
I replied most duly.

"But I fear my contamination
Might blemish you so

As not to tempt damnation,
I persist with the answer, "no."

To have known and lost You --
This I never could bear
So hide, not knowing what to do
Even if for me You truly care.

Then self-inflicted isolation
I suffer in silent despair
Filled with depressive desolation
While You repeat, "I care."

"Why are you stubborn?
You're not some orphan child
But of my own spirit born
Come now to me, child."

(I felt too dirty or contaminated, as if I would
contaminate God. I was in a spiritual quarantine by my
rule, not God's. I could not see He was bigger than my
contamination.)

THE ONE WHO SHARED THE SECRET

Oh! Angelica, my dear Angelica!
Lying beneath the daisies and veronica.
How much I need you now,
To help figure the why and how.

To be able to reasonably discuss it
With someone more than a bit.
And in touch with this pain of yore.
I also need to talk of happiness from before.

(My sister had been molested by my offender and had her own personal experiences, but we only once talked about it before she died.)

MY PRESENT GUILT

My children -- though they drive me crazy,
When my head is full of problems hazy--
I love them more than my life
And because of them, seek solution to strife.

When I scream and wrongly hit,
I worry much more than a bit
As the painfully filling guilt
Makes me wonder if their love I've kilt.

(I really hated these days when I got so overwhelmed
and acted inappropriately. I long for more control and
sought better solutions in counseling.)

TO TRAVIS MY LOVE

Travis, my love,
You can be such a dove,
But also thoughtless.
And maybe senseless.
Hold me my darling.
Make my heart sing.
Tell me you care
As before you didn't dare

I never want to wound you.
For need you, I do.
So come be my love
So we can rise above
This tragic mountain.
Win, thus gain,
That we not falter
And to the devil halter.

(My husband's childhood baggage made it hard for us to
care for each other. We grew further apart when we
needed to be closer. The abuse was the knife that cut us
apart.)

SUBCONSCIOUS EXPRESSIONS

How is it the Lord gives me such strange expression
When I need to bare my soul in confession?
Sometimes in long or short poems,
My mind goes off in subconscious roams.
Or in crying, praying strange-tongued singing
My heart is freed of this painful stinging.

(I sometimes would pray or sing in "tongues". It seemed
to unburden at a subconscious level more than speaking
in English.)

TO EZRA

In the winter of my desolate discontent,
Having bared was not my intent.
But there, all alone and stark,
I faltered in the cool empty dark.

There came a person into my life,
Willingly holding the burdensome strife
So that freed of that great load,
I could better hear what my Lord told.

He made me perceptively aware,
And he showed me worthy of his care,
Proving over and over my importance,
And I need not be victim of circumstance.

(Ezra was my first counselor after I came to terms with
my past events)

IN CONTRADICTION TO HIS LOVE

I stand with the colossal gall,
To sole hold the problems all,
When God Himself had said,
"That by it, I'd be crushed and dead."
So protecting Him from contamination
I held tight without His condemnation
Not knowing the pain in Him inflicted.
And not seeing my thoughts contradicted.
If He is so full of love,
How could He hurt His little dove?.
How foolish of me to hold the pain,
Afraid that such love could ever fain.

(I so often held my pain to "protect" God from the
contamination. His shoulders were bigger and
stronger. I forgot my proper place; He was my
protector.

UNFINISHED BUSINESS

So much unfinished business is your life
That you are driving crazy your wife.
Unfinished house responsibilities and conversations,
They'll still be undone when you are at your final
destination.

(This poem was written in the late eighties. It is now
2018, and not a single room is finished in the house.)

BARED BY THE TALES

I sat naked in your clothed presence,
My silent secrets all exposed;
Everything to you told of every experience.
My greatest fear is you poised,
Ready to run and tell the world
Of my childish sinfulness and guilt.
As I tighten myself embryo-like curled,
Unable to hide behind the wall I'd built.
So tell me now some of your secrets
To help me feel less defenseless.
Even though you say that it's not right,
Seeing in me such selfishness
That you should have to feel that way.
And though I really can't tell more,
Please don't feel you must hold me at bay.
I care enough you may continue your heart pour.
So I'll come back again and do,
Just as you ask and hope
That I can learn to trust, as others do,
And not falter, and leave before I can cope.
Even though I sat naked in your clothed presence,
I'll try hard not to falter and quit my therapy,
But accept you and your nice assurance,
And try hard to smile and not pout.
(This was metaphorical nakedness because I felt so
exposed and vulnerable to my counselor. He said, he
could say nothing about himself; iit would not
professional. It would have been easy to leave
counseling at this point, but I stuck it out. Don't quit just
because you are afraid. Trusting is hard when you've
ACE's. Evaluate the counseling rationally, not
emotionally.)

MY SISTER'S TRUE DEPTH

My baby sister is impulsive and stubborn,
Stiff, board-like, and unyielding since born.
If she knows its white, calls it black,
But not from any intelligence or lack.

She's very much her own individual,
Never hedging from a verbal duel.
Don't ever let her fool you, not once,
Even with head in a cloud she's no dunce.

She has a mind that's very creative,
Though at times it looks only decorative.
She's deep thinking and very insightful,
Living a spontaneous and cognitive life full.

(Later, I found my sister was intellectualizing her
problems, because she wasn't coping with her husband's
childhood baggage. She was too emotionally wounded to
get help and wouldn't ask me to help.)

SICKNESS ON SICKNESS

Illness invaded the soul of me,
Burning through my spirit to eternity.
It seemed it never would end
As sickness on sickness became the trend.
Worn by lack of precious sleep
I was cranky and yell like a creep.

Then my burned-out shell filled of guilt,
And no amount of security built.
Wanting nothing but to wash it away,
I decided it was punishment I must pay.
To be forever lonely in solitary
As the wind blew thru my hull so airy

In this fragile condition I stand;
The wishes of God couldn't understand.
That He called me near Him,
No way I could but hear Him.
I promptly declined the proposition
And did look sharply at my position.

One thing certain, this life was hell.
Then why did I not wish to tell
Him how much I wished to be,
Near to His side instead of flee?
Was my pride in the way,
To cause this abrupt delay?

(Now I was often physically sick and lacking sleep. It
left me less buoyant for healing and less able to accept
help. Most people with long-term stress and distress
have some adrenal fatigue and a compromised immune
system.)

DADDY SAYS

"You dumb and clunky girl."
"Do I have to sit next to you?"
"Do you know what this moving finger is?
An ugly finder that's working."
"So why do you sit and boo-hoo?"
"Because the connection did unfurl."

(Dad did picked on me more than my siblings. Why did
he hate and generally dislike me more? The problem was
I needed to like me more because he really couldn't like
himself.)

ON THAT LANE

On that lane, where I grew,
Between the ancient oak
I took on an awful yoke,
And lessons had quite a few.

On that lane of simple beauty,
Where the grass grew so green
And the clear sky smelled clean,
Praising God was less than duty.

On that lane ending in a lake
Of swimming fish, paddling canoe,
Emerald water refreshing and new,
There did live a fake.

On that lane, across it housed
Friendly, helpful always working,
Secretly, the little girls irking,
Forced silence we all moused.

On that lane, which should be joy,
Filling our childish memories,
Instead, stealing our virginal gemeries,
This man, succeeded in his ploy.

On this lane, now little joy,
From too many sad places,
My life has learned its paces
And other places it's time to employ.
(My safe home turf turned into a scary war zone of
searching for the enemy in a state of constant stress and
hypervigilance.)

MY POOR MOTHER'S FRUSTRATION

My poor Mother's frustration,
When I nightly would wet my bed.
Never would I hold this over her head,
Cuz now as a mother I hold that station
Of changing wet beds and clothes,
And have plentiful dirty diapers toll.
Recycling my mother's frustration,
With a new attitude toward my son.

(I took a different attitude when my son was a
bedwetter; strip your bed, I'll wash it, and then you
remake it. Mom was an angry banshee, like I did it on
purpose. Many children who are molested become
bedwetters. And I was also ADD, another trait that can
lead to bedwetting.)

THROUGH A MILLION TEARS

Onlyness, loneliness
Reach out and touch someone,
Somehow it hurts to think of it.
Though a million tears
Have fallen from my eyes,
They haven't eased my fears.
I tell myself only lies,
And then I try to cry some more.
The truth knowing all along,
It doesn't matter the tears I pour.
I've needed something else for long
To have upon me fall
Just one tear from God.
I'll feel renewed over all
From just one tear of God.

(I felt my tears weren't cleansing my emotional wounds,
but one tear from a saddened God who felt my pain
could heal me if I let Him.)

A MILLION TO ONE

I tried and tried,
And cried and cried.
When a million tears
Took not my fears,
I at last turned
To one spurned
For oh so many
Years if any.
I asked my Father
If He could bother
With a soul
Of such a fool
He said, "Yes,
If I confess
And myself forgive."
The burden given
Over to Him."
So to Him
That thing I did.
Freedom – splendid.
Never thought I
To see eye to eye
With my Father
Who would bother
And a daughter
Who would tauter
But there was I,
Looking in His eye,

Seeing the saving thing.
Something to sing.
Not a million tears,
But only one tear--
The tear of a Father
Who found His lost daughter
Tear of love and joy
And faith employ.

(I had treated a friend badly, pushing her away when she
needed support. Her mother was alcoholic and would
desert her and her siblings for days or weeks. But when I
needed support, she stuck to me like glue, like God
always does. I needed to forgive myself for not
understanding her needs. I also needed to forgive
myself for not being up to my own standards.)

PRAISE TO THE FATHER

No joy has ever filled my heart--
Not one inch, not one part.
Like this, making me dance on air,
Filling my face with something fair.
I have never felt so light,
Never in any day or any night.
What joy! What blissful joy!
A smile easily came my face to employ.
Never need I think of it,
Not even one little bit.
I feel in my eyes ashine
That must give an appearance so fine.
Need I say it? Oh yes, because
My heart overflows; it does.
Truly, truly, I must say the words
Because the praises are my Lord's.
"Praise to You, Oh my God and Father,
The one who cares so much for one daughter.
Praise be always on my tongue,
Even after my time on earth's done.
Praise! Praise! On to my loving Father."

(I grew more distrustful of humans even my family and
leaned on God for acceptance.)

WITH THE DEVIL INSIDE

With the devil inside and God outside,
He wanted me, He wanted me.
With resentment inside and happiness outside,
He wanted me, He wanted me.
With hate inside and love outside,
He wanted me, He wanted me.
With anger inside and peace outside,
He wanted me, He wanted me.
With frustration inside and hope outside,
He wanted me, He wanted me.
With distrust inside and faith outside,
He wanted me, He wanted me.
My God, He wanted me, and
I can feel it, I can feel it.
He wants me to love me.
He wants me, He wants me.
Now with happiness inside and resentment outside,
He loves me, He loves me.
Now love inside and hate outside,
He loves me, He loves me.
Now peace inside and anger outside,
He loves me, He loves me.
Now hope inside and frustration outside,
He loves me, He loves me.
Now faith inside and distrust outside,
He loves me, He loves me.
Now God on the inside and the devil outside,
He loves me, He loves me.
He wants me and He loves me.
He loves me, He loves me.

(Easter Sunday, I could feel the resurrection within
me. Praise God! A change is beginning. I certainly could
feel how great God's love was.)

GOD SEEING ALL

Ashamed of what I was,
Ashamed of what touched me,
And in early years, was
Ashamed of what God would see.

I was told God sees all.
Ashamed of what He'd see,
Sure of the sure appall,
I was ashamed of me.

But God in seeing all,
Saw a part of me
Hidden one and all,
Hidden even from me.

And still loving, He was,
Not ashamed of me,
It is no more, but was
No, I am not ashamed of me.

(I found if I wish to speak from my soul, even poorly
written poetry expresses more than the best prose.)

REMEMBER WHEN

When love comes
Tapping me on the shoulder,
Gently whispering
In my ear,
"Never, never let him go.
He's the one.
Remember how much you love Travis,
How much you've shared together.
Remember how worthwhile the relationship is,
Don't let it slide, work at it,
And for it, it's worth it."

(This proved to be wrong, I was putting all the work, and
he was doing nothing. Or worse yet, he disrupting my
work. I later felt it was more the devil who wanted me
to stay with my husband so I'd never heal and do the job
that was my real life's purpose.)

LOVE YOU

A cup of tea at the bedside,
A note that ends, "Love Travis",
A peck on the cheek,
A call on a business trip,
So many ways to say
"I love you, I love you."
Ways to persevere, to know
Ways to feel.
Touching of two spirits,
The sharing of life as one.
Two as one.

(These rare events were co-dependent manipulations used to keep control and not lose me. It was never about love because he was more messed up than I was. He couldn't understand love; he was just about controlling his environment.)

A SANDCASTLE BE

My life will not a dandelion be,
Blown away and no more me.
But rather, I will be a sandcastle,
Worn by all of life's long hassle
Than ready to rebuild again.
In spite of all of, life may begin.

(I was finding what I was, was not what I had to be
forever. Metamorphosis or evolution as a person is good
with proper evaluation.)

TO DONNA

To water your plants
I would have done,
And gladly so.
But it would seem
Nature had other things in mind.
For it did rain,
Day divided by day,
In the very same pattern
You had instructed.
And plants stayed wet
Without need of me.

But alas and ahem,
I did finally get my chance,
My task to evoke.
For it did stop raining,
So I did as I was told;
Every other day,
Wet and water your plants.

(I was always willing to help other people, and I am to
this day. But I am also am better at seeing when I'm just
being used. Because that happened often, but not this
time. Some molestation victims have boundary issues,
especially about saying no!)

LOVE AND DESIRE

Love and respect grows things
Larger and better.
Wanting and desire shrink,
And after a time
Are no more,
Used up and useless.
Love and respected have
In the meantime
Grown larger,
Fuller, more alive.

(Being used is taking from you. Giving to meet a need is
different. Just don't give it all away so you don't have
anything left for your needs.)

GRANDMA DEAR

Grandma, dear, oh Grandma, dear!
Please feed me!
Grandma, dear, oh Grandma, dear!
Please hug me!

(Grandmas sometimes give love more freely. Moms can sometimes be too busy caring for and doing tasks to just love.)

A PARADOX

Sheltered from the world at large,
Protected in the sweet haven
And yet not safe.
Keep it from her, don't let her know
And yet she felt it
All firsthand
Sunday church and half the other days too.
Wallowing in guilt and shame,
Hadn't really seen the world
Yet knew its hidden secrets.
Couldn't tell a dirty joke
But understood them.
Didn't date till seventeen,
Yet long before understood
Deeper levels of sex.
What a paradox!
So pious and pure
So soiled and shamed.

(My sheltered life kept me from being street smart. It's
not about stranger danger. It's really about a so-called
trusted neighbor or whoever is takes advantage of your
innocence.)

DARKNESS

In the darkness of a shady great tree
Stands the dark toolshed.
Hidden inside are dark memories
Come from dark secrets,
Out of one dark mind
Into another dark recess.
All is darkness from this shed,
Storing dark seeds
To be buried under the dark ground.
Now two are in the dark ground,
Holding the dark secret.
Another remembers in the dark
Or sees with dark eyes.
All is dark in the little shed
Under the dark and shady tree,
Hiding dark secrets.

(The two underground are my younger sister, who was
also molested, and the molester. So only I knew the
secret. This toolshed was the site of the oral sex episode
with neighbor Brock. I was eleven years old. I went to
put Gram's garden tools away when he trapped me. I
was always claustrophobic and afraid of the dark after
that. And the hardware store's smell of grass seed and
fertilizer creeped me out.)

IN THE STILL OF THE NIGHT

In the still of the night,
Sometimes still exists the fright.
Unknowns lurking in the dark,
Frightening the dog into a bark.
Something creeping in murky spots,
Grabbing unsuspecting tots.
Hiding sneaky under my bed,
With heart as cold as the dead.
Where did you come from?
This is really, really quite dumb,
Afraid of nothing or everything.
Every sound making heart ping.
Is it from under the house
Or just a little field mouse?
Maybe from the near heartache,
Kneeling down to look under
The bed; What a blunder!

(This is about the chronic hypervigilance and awareness
of sounds and sights others would never be aware of, but
my fear-filled world was still in my life.)

LOVE TRAVIS

A cup of tea at the bedside
When the morning dawns
A fast scrawled note
Signed, "Love Travis".
Business trips interspersed
With, "Miss you," calls home.
These things and more
Let me know
That you are loving me.

The trip to the grocery store
Coupons in hand.
When my nerves are frayed,
You take the kids
To grandma's house to visit
And return inquiring,
"Feeling better?"
Seeing these in my heart
Lets me know
That you are loving me.

Busy days,
When I need a hand,
Sick days
When I need you to cook,
Lonely days
When I need a friend.
These things and more

Let me know
You are loving me.

Little gifts that come as a surprise,
Even ordinary things,
Some salvaged
Or maybe scrounged,
But something you know
That I might want.
Seeing in my heart
Lets me know
You are loving me.

(Sadly, this was more about controlling me and keeping
me healthy enough to get back to work. I was working
night-shift at the time and not coping well. He also
wanted me up and taking care of him. When I got
bronchitis he never lifted a finger unless it would get him
more later. If he really cared, he'd have stayed home and
done some housework, not gone to his mother's. The
help and gifts were rare and timed. It was mostly wishful
thinking on my part.)

CLEANSED

I looked at the curtains curiously.
Rainwater had left its mark,
A brown and waving line.
All tried, nothing removed it.
Still I tried once more.
Persistence has won;
The curtain is clean.
The right agent to aid the task
Was all that was needed.
I looked at myself; the meanness of
Life had left its mark,
A brown and waving line.
All tried, nothing removed it.
Still I tried once more.
Persistence has won.
I am now clean.
The right agent to aid the task
Was all that was needed.
My Heavenly Father forgives,
And all things are clean as new.

(If your therapy isn't working, don't quit. Look for a
new counselor or a new style of therapy. I used talk
therapy, behavior modification, and group therapy. But
my final step is working the most EMDR (eye
movement, desensitization, and reprocessing). You can
find a style that works best for you. There are many
more types available.)

A TOUCH OF LIFE AND HEALTH

When my babes were young,
Food was not wanting
For to the breast they went.
Joy filled me to know
That the milk of life I fed them.
Just picking them up,
My breast would tingle,
And down the milk would come,
And up they would suck.
So the milk of life gave health.

When someone is ill,
Help is not wanting
For to God they go.
Joy fills Him to know
That the milk of life He feeds them,
Someone else in touching them.
Their fingers would tingle,
And down the spirit would come,
And up they would suck.
So the milk of life gave health.

(Often God uses others as tools of His healing and
feeding our spirit.)

HE TOUCHED ME

He touched me,
He touched me.
Make it go away
Protect me from another today.
It's not that my chest has grown;
To that I'll own,
But if I have a bra,
Just a training bra,
It will be more work
For that old jerk.
To touch me,
To touch me.
In the bathtub,
I'll scrub-a-dub.
I wash yesterday and today,
But it never goes away.
No matter how many bubbles,
He'll be there with more troubles.
He does what he does
Oh! Because of because.
He touched me,
He touched me.

(I asked my Mom to get me a bra because my T-shirt was
too easy for Brock. I also made "Super" bubbles from
hand soap and bubble bath bubbles. I thought the micro
bubbles would clean me better and completely. By the
way, I still hadn't told my Mom what Brock was doing,
because of his threats.)

OF FLYING SNAKES

Gosh sakes.
There are snakes!
Snakes in my bed
Clear to my head!
Big ones.
Little ones.
Roundy round,
And flatsy down.
Every wrinkle
You see a wriggle,
Even a hiss.
And all of this
On the top.
Really, Pop.
The top bunk.
It's not junk.
Gosh, sakes!
They're real snakes!

(With the bedwetting came nightmares of snakes. I was
in the top bunk so Dad said the snakes would have to be
flying snakes to get me. By the way, the bedwetting
followed Brock-episodes. If I told, Brock said he'd go
away and I'd have to deal with snakes while
weeding. He had a deal with Gramp. lf he weeded our
family veggie garden and flower beds on Gramp's rental
property, he got reduced rent on his house.)

CERTAIN NOISES, SMELLS, AND SIGHTS

Slurpy, sloppy, licky noises.
Please dog, stop it!
It reminds me
Of things I don't want to remember.

Fertilizer, raunchy smells
Seeds held without light or ground,
It reminds me
Of things I don't want to remember.

Darkness closing in.
The door, his place,
It reminds me
Of thing I don't want to remember.

(This was about the oral sex in the toolshed. I still can't
stand to hear the dog licking noisily.)

AMNESIA

Amnesia is emotional anesthetic
Worn by each clock tick.
There's no protection from the soul theft
When the remembering is all that's left.

(Repressed memories are targeted amnesia. The worst
part is some of my childhood's good memories get
swallowed with the bad stuff. Brock stole my life in
many ways.)

WET AGAIN

No, Not again
With this busy morning begins,
"You wet your bed
What's in your head?"
"I couldn't help it.
Not one bit."
"Maybe not
You little peepot,
But I've no time
For this sort of grime."
I didn't want to.
That's so.
Waking up wet
And cold to bet
Is not the desire
To which I aspire.

(I wet my bed the mornings after an Brock encounter,
and Mom would always be mad because they
bathroomed me, mostly asleep, at midnight.)

THE TUNNEL

The tunnel, the tunnel,
The winding black tunnel.
Is there an end?
Or was I a fool?
Is it really a cave?
Along maze of a cave,
Not really a tunnel.
What a spectacular joke!
Look for the end,
But there is no end.
No bright and shining end
To all this blackness--
Forever blackness.

(These hopeless periods show up even during therapy.
Sometimes the areas are more deeply repressed because
it doesn't feel safe to remember. EMDR helps. Don't quit
therapy; try another technique, add meditation, prayers,
journaling, yoga, tai chi, aromatherapy, tapping. Just
don't quit. If you aren't healed, the molester is still
victimizing you.)

SUNBEAMS

Children play in sunbeams,
Ill-defined shapes of light,
Changing shapes as they move.
This perspective, that perceptive
Until they are inside it.
Then they feel it.
They know every place it touches them.
They know it's limits.

When we look at God,
Play at the edges of knowing,
Trying to find Him.
Not finding the right perspectives,
But once inside,
You can feel Him,
Knowing everywhere He touches your life
And how you touch others.

(Changing attitudes by changing positions or tactics.)

BABE AT BREAST

He is my baby,
My little Luke,
Sucking at the breast.
Filling with warm milk,
Turned his eyes upward,
Let the breast go.
A smile of recognition
Covering his dear face.
"A-oo", Slipped out.
Then my tear of joy!
Filled with warm love,
My babe feed me.

(The shared experience and recognition of bonding. It's
hard to bond when you can't trust.)

A SPECIAL MOMENT WITH A DOCTOR AND WIFE

How precious is their love?
How very special?
When a husband of so many years
Would be so faithful still
With her so ill,
Reading as she was not able.
A nurse coming upon it
Caught a tear about to flow,
Absorbing this special moment.

TIME TO LEAVE

My cat, my cat,
He misses me,
And I miss him
I'd better get on home.

WHAT THE NURSES SAW

Such a dear,
Such a sweetie.
Gentle lights shine
About thee.
Gentle words of thanks
Spoken to the nurses
For their every action.
Easy to care for.

Such a dear,
Such a sweetie.
Gentle lights shine
About thee.
Air of contentment,
Vision of peace,
Silvered hair shining
Like a halo.
Too soon she'd be an angel.

(The last three poems were about a doctor and his dying
wife. This doctor worked at the hospital when I
experienced this event.)

THE HAT

Arm with needle
Hooked to chemo
On a pole,
Moving down the hall.
Hospital gown flapping,
Revealing glimpses
Of more bottom,
Than should be seen.
Proudly onward,
Smile on his face,
Hat on his head.
All things considered,
"Do you need a robe?"
My Mother dear
Always said,
"You're fully dressed
With a hat on."

SHE'S GOT LEGS

Her patient asks,
"Why always slacks?"
Her pardon begs,
"I've got wooden legs."
Then one day, more or less
She wore a dress,
And the patient spied her
From round a corner.
Seeing her nurse's white legs,
Shouted, "She's got L'eggs,
She's got L'eggs."

(Sad, yet silly encounters with my oncology
patients. They kept me smiling.)

LAWN CHAIRS

The lawn chairs in his yard,
An old-fashion design--
Stiff and metal.
Shell-shaped back;
Painted yellow and white,
Rust and all.
My eyes despise
It's very looks.
I'll sit on it, and
Then I can't see it.

(Little memories can stick around for a long time. I still
avoid that style of lawn chair, but I don't freak out now.)

I HATE HOT DOGS

Hot dogs, hot dogs,
I hate hot dogs.
"Come on, it's okay
To eat it this way."
I gave him a look.
"You must cook it,
Or I can't eat it.
I don't like it."
Looks like a hot dog.
I hate hot dogs.
"Come on, it's okay
To eat it this way."
I gave him a look.
You must be mistook.
"I can't eat it.
I don't want it."

(I now believe that Brock used hot dogs to train his other victims how to approach his penis. I would't be surprised if this is how he trained his own daughter. We later found out he had impregnated her. I'm also glad Mom would't let us eat uncooked hot dogs.)

TOASTED MARSHMALLOWS

"Want a toasted marshmallow?
Your mom will allow,
So what is the harm,"
He asked with viper's charm.
"Come in to my kitchen,"
He'd go on pitchn'.
On a gas-flame toast,
Like a campfire he'd boast.
He'd light the stove
And at my chest dove,
Never getting my marshmallow.
That dirty old fellow
Just lied and lied
Till I thought I died.

(This was his ploy to get me sort of alone in his house,
separated from my mom. This was so he could touch
and suck on my almost breasts. By the way, sometimes
his current wife was in the bedroom and his house was as
tiny as a cottage or the tiny houses of today.

WITH HIS WIFE IN THE NEXT ROOM

Sometimes with his wife
In the next room,
I'd suffer with strife
The accursed doom
That he'd inflict upon me.
Why didn't I yell
Instead of letting it be
And listen to him say,
"Now don't say a thing
Not to anyone!"
All this while quietly feeling
Childhood isn't fun.

(Again this house was unbelievably small. She was in
denial. It turned she had been warned about Brock, but
she couldn't cope with that knowledge. She chose to
ignore her instincts.)

,

DIVING DEEP

Diving into the deep,
Cold and murky waters
Of the past,
Like a scuba cop
Investigating a crime,
Looking for the pieces.
Not able to recognize
What you see.
Broken clues
Rotted with time
Conceal the past.
Hard to recognize.
Should it be tried?
Forensic technology
Is what it needs.
Murky glimpses
Not quite forgotten.
Wish it was
Invisibly hidden
Or else come
Into full view.
It would be easier
To cope with the
Crime of the past.
The mystery I was
Suppose to forget..

(The poem moves fast, like a racing brain. Some gaps confuse and others protect you until you're ready. It's much easier to use EMDR therapy to work through the memories. Other types of therapies help you remember but don't fix the problem. Talk style therapies burn the memories and emotions into the brain's hard drive. That makes the stress more alive and continues to affect your life.)

I KNOW

I love the Lord, I really do.
I know how much He loves me too.
I know how much,
How very much
He could change my life,
Take away all my strife.
But I feel I must be punished a bit
And don't deserve His love one wit.

(It's hard to heal from childhood abuse as long as you
feel like the sinner. I lived in a more innocent time, and
ages seven to eleven were still innocent -- or should have
been.)

I COULD BE

I could be saved
If I was reprieved,
But I don't deserve it.
Sometimes I wish He'd quit
Loving me so
And just go.
Run away from me,
Or contaminated He'd be.

(I had so much trouble accepting God's healing. I felt
like the contaminated leper that Jesus wanted to touch
and heal. But I let my God shrink to my size when I tried
to protect the One who could protect me.)

HE DOESN'T UNDERSTAND

I know the minister doesn't understand.
He just believes me stubborn.
Trying to get God
To come to me,
When all along, I want Him away.
Away where it's safe
Free from contamination.
Just let me go to hell.
I deserve it.

(I felt like a coconspirator because I kept the secret. This
was part of what made me a sinner. This gives more
power to the molester by makes the child feel guiltier.)

I LIKE SCHOOL

There is a reason
Why every season
For school to begin,
Not having to hide in
The house anymore.
I get so happy for
I'd be free to study
Without the old fuddy
Hot on my trail
To catch me without fail
And do those unmentionable
Things I'm not able
To tell to a soul.
But be I fool
Or be I genius,
He can't scare any of us
If we're in school,
Studying at our stool
And desk far away.
The teacher holding at bay
That nasty old man.
Too bad they can't ban
Summer vacation,
When he practices his avocation.
Boy, do I like school
I'm no kind of fool.

(I loved school in spite of dyslexia, dyscalculia and
ADHD problems. And though teachers and students
made fun of me, but anything was better than Brock!)

GIVING UP IS HARD

Giving up is hard
When for years and years,
Your only protection
From molestation
Of body and soul
Was to be in control,
Never giving one inch
To another being
For fear of harm
From snakish charm.
Not ever to man;
More, maybe God can.
I break down
My barriers yet.

(I still avoid any relationships, and not just from
Brock. My parents had a different relationship with me
than my sibs, so they don't understand it either. Trust is
still very hard for me.)

I WANT GOD IN MY HEART

I want God in my heart
And every part
Of my life.
To be a better wife
And mother,
And not just mediocre.
Others ask what can invoke her
To let God in
And so begin
That all new portion
Of a life with devotion?
A life with God first.
Her longest thirst
Finally quenched,
And depression benched.
I must break down walls
And hear God's calls.
Give up all control
Of body, mind, and soul
I know I must.
I could almost bust.
Why can't I do it?
It gives me a fit.
I'm so mad at myself,
My selfish old self.

(Actually, the only being I ever trusted was God. I just
never wanted to contaminate Him. Pretty arrogant and
stubborn when I look back at that attitude now.)

STAND UP FOR YOUR RIGHTS

Inside of me has waged a battle
Between the goodness and the badness.
My head was bowed in shame.
The harder the fight, the more fetal my position.
But God told me to stand up;
Stand up for all my rights.
He placed His hand beneath my chin
And lifted up my face.
My face now to His face,
His eyes intently focused into mine,
He said, "You are born of my spirit,
My own dear child are you.
How could I but love you?"
He paused, then looked with such tenderness
Upon this lowly face.
"Stand up and accept your rights,
My child. Rights that were never denied you.
The right to live your life for Me,
And the right to be loved by Me,
Your God and your Father."
The devil whispers many things
To all us human beings.
He whispers lies and half truths.
Sometimes he says things so uncouth,
You can hardly believe you've heard it.
(This showed some potential shift in attitude. I was now
able to get help to really heal. Also, the healthier we are,
the less control others have over us. Self-esteem is
important.)

CIGARS

Just the smell of a cigar
Can make me cringe.
The stale, old smell
Left on clothes and skin.
He always smoked cigars.
His words smelled of cigars.
His fingers looked and
Smelled of cigars.
Don't smoke near me.
Don't make me smell it--
Old or new, cigar smell.

(For years this smell of cigars, even around a corner,
made me cringe. Now it's just stinky.)

SOMEONE KNEW

Someone knew
And didn't tell.
Someone knew his dirty secret
And told only when
It had known fruition.
Bragged he'd known it
All along.
Could have told the secret,
Saved the shame.
Didn't know it mattered.
Couldn't see the pain.
Contributed to by
Someone who knew
And didn't tell the dirty secret
Till it was caught in progress.

(The owner of a neighborhood business knew about
Brock, but didn't tell Gramp till later when Gramp asked
if he knew anything about Brock. By this time, Brock
had been caught with my sister. He had told another
neighbor with four kids, but he didn't warn anyone else
in the neighborhood.)

SHE KNEW TOO

She knew too.
She must have known.
She made brother buy
Beautiful white bride dolls
For sister and me--
Pure virgin brides--
After purity had left
Sister and me,
And virginity was bruised
A might.

(This was about Brock's second wife. The first wife told
her, and she wouldn't believe that he got his daughter
pregnant, so she said nothing.)

HOW DID MY SISTER FEEL?

How did my sister feel
When her life in a reel
Passed before her eyes,
Knowing more of whys
And wherefores of life
And more of certain strife
Then a young girl should
Know in youth or would
Know if he hadn't stepped
In to her life and crept
Inside her private self
Sneaking, slithering, delft?
Did she die finally free
Of the invasion of her inner me?
Or did she carry onward
Burdened of guilt heavenward?

(My sister only talked to me once after Brock was
caught. She talked about how he showed her his penis
and what it looked like and that was all.)

A FAMILY REUNION

There is a family reunion
That begins with God's union.
More than king or lord,
Separated heavenward,
Instead our own fathers.
We, the sons and daughters,
Accept His special love
Not as a peace dove
But from a father given.
All orphan fears driven,
The devil's lie exposed,
Knowns and unknown supposed
And played upon whenever
Life gives stormy weather.
Like the proverbial brother
Lying he's not your father;
You're only an old orphan.
Your relation made profane,
No hope of full inheritance
Without costly repentance.
Carefully over emphasizing
The product your buying.
Comparing the great cost,
Better inheritance lost
And the devil's won.
A broken family union
Because of his lie

About a price too high.
And you never knowing
That God's love showing
Had no cost connected
Except to God headed.
Climb into His arms
Instead of paying alms.
So join the reunion.
Be with God a union.

(God is the God of relationships. We are His and always
free to come to Him, no matter where our lives have
gone. Methodists talk about prevenient grace, which is
about God meeting us where we are and bring us close to
Him. We can reject or walk away from Him, but His
arms are always open to us.)

MAKE EVERYDAY SPECIAL

Make every day special.
Sing great praises,
Praise to God,
Praise to your family,
Praise to friends and neighbors.
Don't take for granted
Their special talents
To share and make
Your life more fulfilled.
Your praises to others
Make every day special.

(Appreciate life and its blessings. Most LD/ADHD kids hate school. I loved its safe haven so much I kept going to school until I got my PhD thanks to the evader Brock.)

GENETICS AND GOD'S GIFTS

When you're feeling very low,
And you're still rather creative,
With life and death hanging debative,
Remember who is the foe,
Remember who you are,
And the reason you're creative.

(We all have gifts from DNA and life
experience. Expand your gifts; grow and share.)

GLASS TRAP

In the house of glass,
Fire inside,
Devil sits laughing
Knowing the trap well.
Life with pleasure
Close enough to be seen
Yet never touched.
Flames never consuming,
Hell goes on,
On forever, eternally
Heaven on the outside
Only a thought away,
Just a state of mind.
The glass trap is in my mind,
An illusion created.
The devil's hologram,
Or like voodoo,
Believable only when believed.
Believe the truth
And not a lie.
The devil's full of lies,
And there are no traps
Made of glass
Filled with flames.
They're all illusions
From the brain.
Clear your mind.
Free your life.

Let the glass fall away,
And see that the flame
Is only reflection
Of your own fears,
Fed by the devil,
Nurtured by your guilt.
Be free by knowing
God is your Father,
And see heaven
Has no limits
Or boundaries.

(Heaven isn't a place. It is a state of mind, an attitude, a way to live life.)

LIKE A TEENAGER

I feel like a teenager
So out of control,
Emotionally volatile,
Responsibly incapable.
Do I want to be
Free or not free?
By myself, no
Upset by a parent
Over me controlling,
But as much
Afraid of independence.

(Sometimes when you are in the transition of healing, things can get confusing. We aren't completely ready to face parts of the past or present.)

BORN OF SHAME

If there were fame
Born out of shame,
I'd be most famous
With all of the pus-
Filled wound opening.
I'd be better coping
Because of the fame
Born out of shame.

(It can be hard to process stages of emotional wound healing. Skin wounds are so much easier to stage and treat. We should become famous from surviving all of it. There have been suicides from those who couldn't cope to the end.)

I HATE SNAKES

Oh! Pete sakes,
I hate snakes.
I'm afraid to go out in the garden,
So I made a grand bargain.
Before I go there,
I pray a prayer
And believe in my heart
That God will do His part.
Oh! Gosh sakes,
There are no snakes.
Thank You, dear, dear God.
For protecting my scared bod.

(I carried a fear of snakes for a long time. I found God
was a better protector than Brock and more
trustworthy. If the snakes showed up, God gave me
courage greater than fear.
This also shows how much Brock fed and fixed my fear
of snakes.)

WHEN LOSING CONTROL

When I'm losing control
And feeling a fool,
God says, "Pray."
"But what do I say?"
Then He tells me that
And gives me a pat,
"Get on with your life
For there is no strife.
When I share the burden,
You have less stress on
Your shoulders to carry.
Together, life is less scary."

(I do what I call step prayers. I first pray about what to pray for to narrow the focus. This process sorts out the garbage in a stressed brain. Then you know how to pick and focus the important issues because the worry and fear list shortens.)

BROCK

Brock. Brock, what you did.
Brock. Brock, what you said.
Did you realize the harm
When you used your charm
To take advantage
Of my preteen age?
Or was your own pain
So great that my pain
Meant nothing or less?
What would you confess
Of childhood experience?
Let's not words mince.
Was your childhood the same?
Were you a victim of maim,
Maim of your soul?
Did it take its toll?
Your past guilt and sin
By repeating again and again
These acts against me
And my sister be,
Or didn't you ever think
You'd fill of our lives
With such burdensome strives?
Brock. Brock, what you said.
Brock. Brock, what you did.
(I wonder what kind of childhood could create such a
monster as Brock. Why you didn't change your course
by other choices instead of assaulting so many others by
your bad deeds.)

SHAME, SHAME ON YOU

Shame, shame,
Shame on you.
Tongues clucking and wagging,
Fingers pointing and shaking.
Shame, shame,
Shame on you.
You make a mistake on homework.
Didn't cross the street right.
Wet your bed again.
Gave the wrong answer.
Couldn't hit the ball.
Couldn't ride your two-wheeler.
Look so ugly and gawky.
Let him touch you
Then touch you again.
Shame, shame,
Shame on you.
Tongues clucking and wagging
Fingers pointing and shaking
Shame, shame,
Shame on you.

(I needed to quit ripping on myself for every little
nothing that happened. This was a clue that I had poor
self-esteem.)

OF ROCKS AND ISLANDS

So heavy with shame and guilt
I can hardly move.
I feel like a rock.
But a rock is safe,
Free of emotion,
Doesn't go too far.
They say, "No man is an island,"
But that's too bad.
Islands are safe.
They don't have to act
Certain ways
Or interact with any other land,
But man must do that.
This is so unsafe,
So very unfair.
For there are no signs on a man
To tell their intentions,
To warn you of danger.
There are no types of man
Like rocks,
Whose quality and character
Are known
Instantly on sight.

(Too bad people don't have warning signs like, "I'll use
and abuse you, and then make you feel bad about
yourself." So trust your gut. If it gives a little twist,
something isn't safe.)

HATE

Oh! Hideous hate
That corrodes and corrupts.
As a destructive tool.

(Don't let another's hate be yours or let treatment or
attitudes become your hate or anger.)

COUSIN TO COUSIN

How could you turn your back on me?
I'm so happy to see you.
I've had to play with just my brother
And all week at that.
Cousin, Oh! Cousin
Aren't you happy to see me?
Now don't tease.
Play with me, please.
I wanted to see you.
Don't you want to see me?

(People can be oblivious to other's feelings; it is easy to be hurt. But remember most of them don't get it. Most don't know how hurtful they are being unless you tell them. We aren't a race of mind readers.)

NOT WORTHY

Why can't I feel worthy to do it,
To give up this burden
Too heavy for me to carry?
Just cut away cold-turkey
Leaving all behind,
All that causes sadness,
All that causes illness.
Am I really so bad
I deserve the punishment
Of not knowing His grace,
To not be near His love?

(I wrote this about what my mind set was before I had a Gestalt fantasy journey which brought about some real movement toward healing.)

JANUARY 1986

Strange and haunting January thaw.
Such are the things I felt as I saw
Teasing traces of snow
Interlaced with tingling taunts of grass.
Happiness mixed with sorrow,
Knowing so soon snow would come again.
Bare trees reaching in waving arms
Into a crisp, gray-blue sky,
Praying, God have mercy please,
And let spring begin for the trees
Not just in jest.

(Cold and stark as winter was my heart. I longed to grow
green and hearty like the trees.)

WINTER WIND

Heavy hand on the harp,
  Puck the pale ply,
While wild winter wind
Makes mournful music.

Silent snow-shed sky,
Blanketing the black night,
While wild winter wind
Makes mournful music.

Cold, crisp character,
Till temperature in teens,
While wild winter wind
Makes mournful music.

Icy inlaid interstate,
Crawling, creeping cars,
While wild winter wind
Makes mournful music.

Regular random, radio-like,
Sounds sing strangely,
While wild winter wind
Makes mournful music.

Tiny twigs twining,
Rattling in racing rage,

While wild winter wind
Make mournful music.

Power ploughed piles,
Snow stacked steep,
While wild winter wind
Makes mournful music.

Four-wheels ford forward,
Downs dangerous drifts,
While wild winter wind
Makes mournful music.

Whole world white
In icy isolation,
While wild winter wind
Makes mournful music.

(We went to visit out-of-town relatives and got snowed in by a sudden blizzard. The wind made strange sounds on the TV antenna's support wires. I scribbled this baby on scraps of paper, because the poem begged to be written.)

TORN IN PIECES

Why must He let me climb so high
Only to push me down?
The pieces grow harder to glue together;
The shreds become to fine.
I grow too fragile to try.
Soon I will be buried in my own depression.
No more will I grow
On the edge of existence.
But tears falling as heavy as rain
Change things.
Watered by despair,
New growth comes out of old.
New directions taken,
Drawn by the touch of the Son.

(Sometimes therapy doesn't make problems go away it
makes it small enough to examine more closely or deal
with them. Just gluing pieces back together doesn't
constitute healing. Sometimes even emotional wounds
need debridement to truly heal.)

ALICE OF THE LOOKING-GLASS

For all too many years
Filled with unbelievable fears,
I looked and saw
And did the wrong conclusion draw.
For it was his reflection,
Given with his false detection,
An ugly image
There too long an age.
The sight has so much lack
From the mirror side black,
Not seen ever with my eyes
But only through his lies.
I peer insecure
At a picture pure.
There on the other side
Is a face I can abide.
The true reflection
Of his so-called affection
Without his evil lies.
There are pretty blue eyes,
Shiny golden hair;
At this beauty I dare stare.

(My husband's insecurity and need to control caused
him to call me, "ugly," "fat," "stupid, "or whatever else
came out of his mouth. My poor self-esteem accepted
his judgement because I believed it was true. One day I
looked in the mirror and saw me as I actually was. It was
a step toward change. A new path of evolution.)

ALONE WITH LONELINESS

Aloneness can be coped
For it is always hoped
An end will come.
Out and away from
Self you can go,
At will can go.

But loneliness is stark
There is no rainbow arc,
So much blackness,
Escapeless bleakness,
Self is empty.
No place ready.

Aloneness can be chosen
Even when you have been
There a great time.
It can be prime.
If you chose,
You don't lose.

But loneliness is stark,
A sad and crying lark
Wintered in isolation.
One in revelation.
So little hope,
One can't cope.

Aloneness with God,
And you can plod
Life's path unafraid.
For Jesus bid,
"Follow me,
Saved you'll be."

But loneliness is stark
There is no rainbow arc.
No one near,
No one dear,
God walled away
Thinking it safe to stay.

Aloneness can be healing,
Allowing all feeling
In concentrated confusion,
Allocated correct perfusion,
Carefully selected,
Personally elected.

But loneliness is stark,
So empty and dark,
Grabbing unseen
Emotions mean,
Fear or delusion,
Anxiety or depression.

(You can chose to wither in loneliness or grow healthy.
In quiet meditation, you can direct your thoughts and
attitude toward healing and refreshing.)

GHOSTS

I am the ghost
Of ages past.
An ethereal host
Of emptiness.
Fill me up, Lord.
At long last
With joy poured
To fullness.

(The true cause of feeling empty can sometimes come from a cleansed emotional wound. You aren't filled with the infection and inflammation that make up emotional wounds. This can mean you are ready to fill up with positive emotions instead of negativity and depression.)

! ! ! FREE ! ! !

Free, I am free
To serve my Lord,
No longer under the Controller,
Not dominated by his wishes.
Stressed by stress,
Dominated by depression,
No more.

Free, I am free
To serve my Lord.
Servant of God, yet free man.
His wishes mine.
The yoke of distress
His to carry, not mine.

Free, I am free
To serve my Lord.
To sing His praise,
To glorify His name and ways,
His needs to address
In service to God, yet free.
Finally free to chose.

(Buckling under to a controlling partner, drugs, or
depression is like becoming an idol worshipper or part of
a controlling cult. Heal to choose your life path as a
whole person.)

FOR BETSY

What for a friend we could,
Even though for self should,
We do for a friend.
Great reaches of energy,
Knowledge searched to the end.
A God known beyond liturgy.
Helpful words of knowledge,
Networking God's clues.
God-reliance acknowledges
There is no way to lose,
When for a friend we could
And through it for self would.

(My friend had mental health problems but somehow
controlled them enough to research help for me, like
Bible verses and books, but never quite saved or healed
herself. Sadly, she was controlled more by her delusions
and had less healing. And she broke her family with
abuse born of delusions.)

DESPAIR

I can't see past the despair
And don't seem to care.
Caught in a pit,
I don't like it a bit.
"Tunnel out!"
They shout!
And I just pout,
Raining tears,
Drowning in fears
In that pit;
I don't like one bit.
Maybe I'll float,
If they don't gloat.
Get out of there!
In the well of despair,
Tears can drown
Or slip on a frown
And never come up.
Die quite abruptly,
Filled with despair
When you don't care
How you fare.

(When you're still healing and progress gets slow, you
may want to give up to despair. Change something it's
scary, but productive, because what you're doing isn't
working now. Change the counselor or the type of
counseling. Change can start new emotional healing like
debriding a skin wound.)

EMOTIONAL DEATH

All I could wish
To fantasize and dream about
Is to go to sleep,
To sleep on undisturbed.
Pull the dirt up around my ears.
At last be one with the earth.
No more to move separate,
Alone in my small
And purposeless circles.
When my body is cold,
I will not feel the cold of the earth.
One by choice with parasites,
Not picked as prey,
Life sucked out day by day.
Trampled upon and abused,
Death of emotions, feelings, senses.
There is so little life in me.
Let me find rest;
I am too weary to cling.
Life is too full of parasites
Who would steal your life force.

.

Breathe life into me, Oh! Yahweh,
That I may not live beneath the earth.
Too soon this end would come--
Never having purpose,
Never feeling worth.
Precious heavenly Father,

Fill me up with your will.
Lighten my burden dear Christ.
Let me move forward
To your will and purpose.
Let my life glorify your name.
Renew those parts deadened in me.
Love me
That I might know worth.
Take the burden from me
That tires for death,
Pluck off the parasites
That gnaw my flesh.
I chose You
Because You have chosen me.
I don't understand your love,
But I cling to it
For Your love fills me up
It is all the life
That exists in me.
Without You, great God,
I am nothing;
I am as the dead.

(Low self-esteem can lead to poor partner choices which
can destroy further hunks of a small esteem. Depression
was drowning me until, divorce would throw me a life-
saver. Hubby kept picking my wounds to keep me sick
and weak. He was one of the emotional parasites picking
at me.)

NIGHTMARE CAGE

Nightmare fears
Caged me in too small.
Poked and prodded,
Nowhere to escape.
Jailor's joy;
Knowing I'm trapped,
He pokes and prods.
Nowhere to escape.
Filled with fears,
Frustration, and anger.
Trapped too tightly,
Bars too small,
Cage too small,
Tears fall fast.
Jailor laughs.
Paralyzed by hopelessness,
Trap of no escape.

(This is me screaming for the courage to get a
divorce. The marriage was an unhealthy environment. I
was having nightmares about being trapped underwater
or being held down.)

TO JUSTIN

There is an empty spot
For one I knew has gone.
He fought the long, hard fight
As a brave soldier of life.
While he yet lived,
His joy spilled out on others.
Brown, dancing eyes,
And smiling lips,
Incited others to happiness
And an energy to live.
Sensitivity and caring coaxed
Hopeful thoughts in others.
Oh! empty spot,
Fill with memories
Of a good man who shared life
And bravely fought its battles.

(Justin died in the spring of 1993 from complications of
juvenile diabetes and heart failure at age forty-one.)

TRUST

Oh! Divine and faithful One,
You promise us our needs met.
Why do we wear ourselves
To shreds with worry?
You are there, great Jehovah,
With your watchful eye
And loving heart.
You know our limits
And satisfy our needs.
But that we could trust
And dare to hope,
One-tenth the energy expended
On loathsome worry.
We would then have peace . . .
That special promise . . .
The peace that passes understanding.

(During my divorce, I lived the trust and praise in the
hymn - "Great Is Thy Faithfulness". I was away from
family, friends, home, car, and money and even physical
health, but God kept providing. I came to understand
God better and trust more.)

HAPPINESS' HORIZON

So many roads down
Deep in depression,
Lonely in withdrawn isolation.
The wind and dust of life in my face.
How will I know,
Know the way to find happiness?
So many years separated,
Will I recognize its surroundings,
Know its signs?
Clouds lift away
As the road veers at an angle.
With the sun on my face,
My heart is warmed with hope.
Life has moved suddenly
And wonderfully upward.
There is lightness in my step and
Peace in my mind.
This is the long-sought treasure.
This is happiness.

(I believe that this was the sign that my decision to
divorce was correct. Staying with him was just scab
picking, hoping for healing. I knew deep down no
healing would happen in that marriage.)

TO MARGARET

Thank you, Margaret,
For being God's unwitting tool.
You're given me the fuel
To stand again.
When I was too weak to care,
You spurred me on
Without a con.
So now I can bear
To face my trouble,
Not as a mere prisoner,
But with the help of my strengthener.
Freed from your bubble,
You had done it alone.
So with my great support system
Of friends and God's kingdom,
I succeed not alone
But with a great force
Holding me upright.
My abusers to indict
On this new life course.
Thanks again, Margaret,
For your fine model
Of all that I'll do.
Thanks for your acumen.

(Margaret went through abuse and encouraged me to get
free, assuring me it was possible.)

HERE'S TO YOU, DION !

Drink became your cherished focus;
Everything else stood in the way.
Work, wife, and children,
New infant, about one each year.
Alcoholic and workaholic,
Never time for family.
Cash a paycheck at a bar,
Spent on so many rounds.
Urged by, "Do it again, Dion!"
Anger welled in stupid impulsivity,
Knowing inadequacy as a provider.
Children starving saved by the mother,
Anger grows cuz she can do it.
He can't.
Defuse the paradoxical guilt
With fist blows and angry words.
Sometimes a revolver.
Hidden inadequacies
Poured out in putdowns.
Belittled wife made a stepstool
For your step to superiority.
Hurt and in pain, she grows bitchy.
Dion need never touch the kids.
His anger outpours,
Flows mutant madness
Through his wife's suffering.
All look confusion filled.
Who's the abused, and where's the abuser?

Dion's making another round of
Vicious cycles of abuse.
Where even a victim looks villainous,
Deceptive, friendly hero by day,
Nasty inflictor of pain by night.
As the true hero
Holds her world together.
With increasingly weak arms,
She holds desperately her kids.
She doesn't feel enough worth
To do it for herself.
While Dion determinedly pulls apart,
"Play it again Dion," and,
"Here's to you."
The great debilitator of
A decimated family,
Now that mutant goo
Of traumatic pain, and lashing anger
Pours forth by your dishonor
On your son's family,
Wife and children.
Start a new round,
So even though you're dead,
"Play it again Dion" for
"Here's to you".

(My husband's family was a quagmire of toxic emotional
waste. Alcoholic, bipolar, abusive father and angry,
bitchy, physically and mentally beaten mother.)

TRAPPED

Trapped by unfulfilled needs,
Maureen, I see your pain
In tight pinched lips
That hold back the truth.
Facts, not fiction of suffering.
You didn't have
Books or support groups or family
To help you back then.
It was your job
To grin and bear it.
But the burden was many times greater,
And you punished yourself
As you eased the pain with food.
You complained and whined
Of trivial things to offset
Your hopeless, uncontrollable world,
Where nasty words
And stinging hands
Were poor substitutes for love.
And loneliness was averted
By belonging to a family
Of secret tortures.
You were trapped by shame.
Trapped by guilt and need.
The self-esteem you needed
Was knocked out of you,
Locking the door on the cage--
Never to be fulfilled,

Never knowing how brave you were, or
How worthy of so much better.

(This was for my mother-in-law. She was trapped
because Catholic families of this time were just expected
to keep having babies and stay married-- even with an
abuser. He was unfaithful and emotionally and
financially neglectful.)

TORTURED LIFE

When the loneliness
And pain of depression
Fill you up to overflow,
Even wishes are torture.
Suicide end and
Cancer termination
Ends the pain.
Not dreamed of gradual decline,
But soon,
Finalizing emotional hurt.
The suffering has
Gone on so long.
Must the end go so slowly?
Finally free from torture,
Make it fast.
Take it from me.
Dear Jehovah,
Take my pain.
Take my burden.
Let me know freedom.
Peace that passes understanding.
Too long I've suffered.
I call on you.
I need your aid,
I can't survive without you,
Great Jehovah.
Save this, your slave.
Take the torture, and
Leave the life.

(My depression got greater until I filed for a divorce. In
some way, my will to live for my sons and depression
predivorce actually gave me increased my strength to
live.)

TRIBUTE TO SELF-HELP BOOKS

Surrounded by books--
Walls of books--
Books for healing,
Books for recognizing,
Books for skinnizing,
Books in my face
And all around my feet.
Books including
Not enclosing
In a prison of fear and pain.
No! Books are my heroes,
Surrounding with protection.
Self-helping in direction
I'm ready to receive.
I'll use these books as steps--
A wall of steps--
To get out of my imprisoning pit.
These offerings of love
By heroes, many who have found
Themselves in painful pits.
So they give help
Page by page,
Forming steps of rescue.
Thanks to my heroes,
I'll repay you by helping another
With your books of self-help,
And someday, maybe my own

As a tribute to the legacy
Of mute paper
That, through printed words,
Can cheer us to hope and help.

(This tribute to self-help books will be my song of
courage to write books to help others. My steps to a new
life then a new career, healing beyond the walls of a
hospital, into homes of hurting lives.)

VAMPIRE'S VICTIM

I once was a pretty girl,
Slender and healthy
But flawed,
With low self-esteem.
This marker laid me victim
To the predatory parasite.
He injected me with the digestant:
Insults, half-truths,
And backhanded compliments,
Sometimes silent withdrawal.
With this liquefying breakdown,
He could manipulate and control,
Sucking life out of me.
Work on my guilt or shame,
Master my goodness.
Suck out more life,
Withdraw in his relation,
Repressed his emotions,
Isolated even in togetherness.
I collapsed in depression.
He descended upon me
To suck out yet more life.
Too little left to survive.

(My broken husband used me as a scapegoat for his pain,
sucking life and happiness out of me. He had so much
emotional damage from his toxic childhood.)

DIRECTIONS

God promises He'll give us
Only what we can handle.
If that is true, and
I believe it's so,
How do we decide
What gets ignored
Except by prayer?
Talk to the great, All-knowing One.
Then listen quietly.
Know He is handling
The unmanageable tasks
According to our measure,
Always leading us to
Tools prepared for our tasks.
Starts with the instruction
Manual called the Bible.
Then prepare a clean work space,
Accomplished by confession and forgiveness.
Understand the directions
By clarifying prayer;
Accept help from directed sources.
These are God's tools too.
With faith, hope, and trust,
Hold firm to the task
Till it is done.

(I have felt God's directions often in my life. He led me
to cities, schools, doctors, and counselors. He hasn't
failed me. He never left me without a healer, food,
clothes, or home.)

CINDER CITY

Burnt out from depression--
And yes, loneliness too--
From my own secret past,
Sexual contact on my
Much too young body.
Fired in shame and guilt.

All along burnt-out wifedom
Yet mother to a perpetual son,
Too emotionally wounded
To understand wholeness,
Because of his painful past,
Which inflames my life also.

Burnt out from my job.
Too many years of cancer dying
And wheezing, pain-filled patients.
Too much giving of self
To terminal people.
Death and pain were my companions.

Then, kid burnout happened.
Too-serious and colicky boy
Conflicts with impulsive one.
Invading forces on precious calm.
Hyperactive mouth and body
Confronts quiet, still son.

So off to cinder city I go.
All burned on every side.
Stoker spouse throws on fuel,
Keeping the home fires burning.
Burnt out wives are better.
They are so much more manageable.

Cinder city I have arrived.
Sizzling with serious anger,
Turned inward to depression,
I've burned out and up.
Black, crusty, crispy cinder.
Burnout's certain victim.

(This was about husband burnout, work burnout, kid
burnout, and me burnout. I needed a vacation from life.)

3 BULLETS IN THE FLOOR

Past-life anger filling up,
Alcohol and lead poisoning,
Mind toxified and unreasonable.
Lashing out in severe pain,
Threatening self-extinction
While pointing a gun at others.
Fear filled room,
Conflict fills to the corners.
Words deciphered as a weapon.
Gun aimed at the head of the one who talked.
But God and pregnant sister intervened.
Three bullets are in the floor,
Not in my forehead by God's grace.
Nurturing this needy person.
God's gift of forgiving filled my heart.
This is beyond, most surely from God.
Loving talk and warm hugs,
Are still there for this person.
Where there would be human hate.
There is love
By God's gift of forgiveness.

(This is from a February 1981 incident at my sister's
home, which I am lucky to share, because the three
bullets were for my forehead. I had come at my sister's
request to help my brother-in-law. Ask me what I think
about stronger gun laws? ! ? Yes, yes,yes !!!)

DROUGHT OF "93"

The poor, dry earth,
Parched and thirsty.
Grass so dry it
Breaks and blows.
Trees so dry that
Leaves flutter and fall,
In August,

Teasing storms pass by
With noisy acclamation,
But no water falls.
Fine mists fill the air,
Yet only a few drops come down.
With every wind that blows,
A cloud sends hope,
But the earth remains dry.
Hopeless in silence,
The ground waits.
There is nothing else to do.

Mute and still, but
God knows earth's need.
Started with one fast
Little drink.
Then a long dowsing,
Thorough and deep.
He knows the need and
Gives the care.

(This paralleled my personal life at the time. I was at my
new home away from my husband, family, and friends.)

I AM A PERSON

Years and years passed,
And I moved about as unnoticed
As a shadow.
I was a non-entity.
I existed to no one
And for no purpose.

Then a small ray of hope came;
Someone needed me.
I moved up the evolutionary ladder.
I had progressed to an object,
Something for my abuser to use.

But one day I stretched further upward.
Became assertive, independent,
Took on life without being needed.
I had moved for enough
To be a person.

(My new life as a person, began after I moved away from
my husband and only because I moved away. I was
determined to grow as a person.)

ANGER

Anger surrounds me like a circle of fire.
Threatening to burn me all away.
Anger for failures--
Job, marriage, and children.
Anger for abusers--
Brock, Dad, and Travis.
Anger for helpers--
Mom, counselors, and ministers.
Anger for losses--
Childhood, home, and marriage.
Anger for me,
Always less than I could be.
The heat of this anger
Burns my flesh.
Cheeks reddened and blistered.
Flames raised to such heights.
Anger can be consuming
When you are lost in its
Flames of destruction.

(Anger was the fuel source of my energy that moved me
on to new pathways. Otherwise, I would have burned up
in the flames of depression. Plus, school filled many
spaces in my mind that could have fueled more anger. I
have a pattern of going back to school when stressed.)

I BELIEVE IN ME

What if a duck didn't believe he could float?
Would he have to have a boat?

What if a bird didn't believe he could fly?
Would he need a plane to get up in the sky?

What if a horse didn't believe he could trot?
Would he need a car to get from spot to spot?

What if a fish didn't believe he could swim?
Would he use a submarine when going upstream was his
whim?

(This is an older poem that was part of a story, but it fits
where I was at the time. This is a reminder to believe in
yourself and use your talent for their best
purpose. Know yourself, really know yourself to
believe.)

GORE ORPHANAGE

Without stars or moonlight,
In the cold and creepy night,
Down the swervy, curvy road,
From the huge orphan's abode
Came the bloodcurdling cries.
Flames consuming in vain tries.
Many young lives the cost,
Ghosts forever in limbo lost.
So was the tale of Gore Orphanage,
Cries still heard throughout an age.

(I wrote this as an introduction to a short story for a
writing class about a local legend. The fire actually
happened many years after the orphanage closed, but
boys used the story to coax girls to this infamous necking
site: "I'll hold you tight, so you'll be safe.")

SOME FUN LIMERICKS

THE FLOWER MAN

I once knew a man so willowy,
Who reached over the fence reallowy,
With a big red zinnia,
"For your mother, ninna,
And for you a tale so sillowy."

(This was a about a nice trustworthy neighbor, that I
wanted to honor him as someone special.)

There once was a girl named Lucy,
There never was such a dosy.
She was a great bully,
So wild and wooly.
She could even beat a big moosey.

There once was a baby named a Kent.
He got himself all twisted and bent.
To untwisted he could,
And unbent he did good,
And all without leaving a dent.

There once was a young boy called Weston.
To start reading his choice not to hasten.
So at the age of four,
At a time well before,
He was even in school a season.

There once was a toddler called Jordan.
From a baby, he was anything but thin.
His body covered with muscles,
With his brother sometimes he tussles,
At weight lifting, he someday will win.

There once was a girl named May Lee,
She said, "I want to dance, truly."
So on went her ballet,
Without any delay,
And for her hard work, a job she got duly.

There was a young girl called Casey,
Who picked all flowers, but the daisy.
Asked her mother," why?"
To this she did reply,
"By the time, I picked the others I felt too lazy."

There was a big boy named Abbott,
Who was handsome even as a tot.
He could steal your heart
Before you could part.
So others would know it, the words I did jot.

Carol, the girl had been named.
Of doll playing, she was famed.
A Barbie, Ken, and Polly,
And even a baby dolly.
All to be dressed was her goal aimed.

There once was a young lady named Pamee.
On the boys she'll soon put a whammy.
For at her they look,
And for her they took
A box of fine candy made by Sammy.

There was a girl called Carrie,
Who loved all fruit, especially the berry.
Their juicy sweet taste,
She never would waste,
Eaten always on ice cream from the dairy.

There was a young girl named Ebony.
She once went to an island called Coney,
All for the sake
Of a hot dog to take
Home because she didn't like a grocery phoney.

(I embroidered the limericks and some corresponding
pictures as wall-hangings for Christmas presents for all
the cousins.)

Back to the journal, I thought you might need a break
from the heavy stuff.

COLOR COMES TO MY WORLD

One drizzle down,
Hum-drum day.
When seasons end,
Bespoke of fallen leaves.
Where moist world
Turned gray bark black.
In this colorless world,
I found a surprise.
Tandi, Hope, and Dorcia!
They came for craft projects,
Bare shirts in hand.
"Colors, paints!" they screamed,
"We need them bright!
Red, blue, yellow, and green!
Shirts for our father's,
Their birthdays, you know.
Colors! Beautiful colors!"
But even without their pretty paints,
These bright and joyful girls
Brought color into my day.
No more gray and colorlessness.
Thank you! Special children!
Thank you! For the joy you bring!

(I was healing here enough to recognize joy and it
colored my world. I'm happy again.)

BLUE CHRISTMAS WRAP

Depression wraps my heart
And foils my eyes.
But from what store
Is this depression bought?
From Dad's bah-hum bug?
From Travis's week late presents?
Deeper in the storehouse ---
To the unlovedness,
To the unwantedness.
Clearly marked on the sign,
No sale!
Too high a price
For your perverted presents.
No more heart wrapped with
Depression.
I am worthy of a gift
That symbolizes worth,
Not just an empty box
Or mere junk from the trash.
Acknowledge my worth,
Show me I'm wanted.
With thoughtful, timely picked presents,
Not of monetary worth,
But heart worth.

(I was seeing the source of my painful depression was
the way I was treated; it told me l was worthless. It fed
and validated the storyline of my low self-esteem.)

LORD OF LIGHT

Lord of Light,
Fill my gray days
And dark ways
With your presence.
Lift me up from the pit,
Away from darkness,
Sadness, brokenness.
Hold me up
With hope,
Hope healing the brokenness,
All the cracks and tears.
Then fill me with faith
So I can cling
Strongly and firmly
To Your ways
In all my days.

(I saw where my healing was coming from:, it was the
faith and hope to heal completely.)

Wish list
For the season
Of forgotten reasons.
Christmas wish list full
Of what?
Some may ask for toys, gadgets, and such,
Trying very hard to fill their empty lives.
But when you are so very broken,
These many great things fall out.
Instead take God's gift of
Unconditional love
And acceptance
Jesus Christ
Is yours
Now
*

(This poem addressed the mixed-up way we in America
looked at Christmas in the 1990's.)

SHUT DOWN

My mind is so busy,
Yet nothing is there.
I race inside.
Yet I am too tired for my body to move.
What am I to do?
Which is the true way?

Sit silently;
Let all run down.
Sit silently;
Listen to the Lord.
Sit silently;
Let only your spiritual ears function.

No energy is needed
Passivity is trust.
All is with the Lord
For He will show the path.
He will fill you with proper energy.
He will say when to move.

(Burnout keeps you from thinking clearly. Rest, listen
and let God take over. Then you'll move in the right time
and at the right speed.)

RELENTLESS LOVE

Oh God! Great and Sovereign Lord,
I praise you for your relentless love.
When our pain is so great we flee,
You surround us,
Protecting, cherishing.
Praise for a love so caring,
So inclusive in its unconditional nature.
Relentless love, I claim You,
Fill me up now
For I accept You.
I will run no more.

I pray Great Yahweh,
That You make abusers Your prey.
Chase them down relentlessly.
Surround them in their pain.
Let them know Your unconditional love.
I praise You for I know,
Even as I ask,
You start this work
Long before it is deserved.
You loved my abusers
Even as they push You away.
Your love is relentless.

(God's love doesn't forget or lose us. Victims and
abusers are both worthy of healing.)

THE BRIDE OF FRANKENSTEIN

The bride thought she was being
Draped in lace
For her wedding.

Little did she know they were
Sterile drapes
For a frontal lobotomy.

Don't give it a thought,
My dear, just
Do as you're told.

Work a full-time job,
Pay the bills,
Clean the house.

Read my mind, so I get
What I want
Before I say it.

Don't give it a thought,
My dear, just
Do as you're told.

Caught in the trap, lobotomized,
Can't remember
How or why.

My mind has been cloudy
In a veil
Since my wedding day.

(I was still clearing out pain and emotional wounds from
my marriage. It is less often, but sometimes rants flush
out the old wounds.)

SYMPHONY OF SYMPATHY

I have seen your pain
Written in your sad eyes
And furrowed in your forehead.

I have seen your fatigue
From a battle long fought
In your gentle and labored voice.

I have seen the depth of your problems
In the silence, holding your secrets
In sterile emotional periods.

I have seen the confusion of healing
In the struggle for acceptance of others
And even of the healing.

I have seen your struggle with boundaries in
How much of a load to take
And how to avoid pain again.

I have seen your anger with God
In the lonely looks
And the walls you build.

I have seen your heart and soul
It has touched points of my pain
I pray for your healing as my own.

(I could more easily see others pain after I faced my own
pain and woundedness. Then I could pray and help them
heal.)

ASHLEY'S POEM

Why God? Why
Did you leave me alone?
I God, I
Needed You.
Why God? Why
Didn't You save me?
I God, I
Needed You !

He touched me when and where he wanted.
God where were You?
Didn't You see what wasn't wanted?
God where were You?
And what about my mother, Lord?
God where were You?
Her words cut like a sword, Lord?
God where were You?

Ashley, I your God was there.
But your father could not,
Would not hear me.
He chose another's message.
Your mother was too wrapped
In self to know My voice.
And you, dear Ashley,
Kept putting up walls
Made of blocks of hate, anger, and despair.
You blocked me out when I, your God,
Could have helped you most.
Break down the walls dear child,
I am there waiting to protect you,
More powerfully and knowingly
Than mere walls.
(A friend's healing halted by not seeing God's presence
and the limits set by the human's free-will.)

JOY'S SACRIFICE

From out of the past
A secret, superstitious ritual
Born of an alcoholic family.
With a blistering halt
To emotions
Came the symbolic death of joy,
Squelching any happiness.
Kill any peace.
Don't let it happen.
Spy on the reactions of others.
Sabotage if you must.
Don't allow joy
Beyond the sacrificial altar.
Drive the knife of unhappiness
Through its heart.
Sprinkle the blood
Born of despair
Onto all.
Go about your life
Shrouded in the traditional garb--
The weeds of death,
Death of joy.
Wail in the dark and lonely night.
Mourn all hope of happiness.
Don't allow the new born
Child of marriage
To let joy slip in;
Sacrifice it too.
Carry on the joyless
Alcoholic family ritual,
All joy and happiness
Thrown on the altar.
(This was yet another damaged person from childhood
sexual abuse.)

HEADACHES WITHOUT END

In the fleeting moments of joviality,
My son's pun, a joke on TV,
I grab for life in the mire of depression.
Depression, thick and deep as death.
Will I ever find happiness?
Two years these severe headaches
Have squeezed my brain
And laid me flat.
For only flatness relieves the pain.
Not the surgery, not any medicine,
Only flatness.
So little life exists from a couch
Or bed
And that all too frequent pain
When I arise.
A coffin seems a better answer;
You don't arise from that.
And surely death's numbness
Wipes out all the pain.
How can I be a student?
More yet, a worker?
A mother?
My life is confined to a two by six
Ever flat existence.
A coffin is not so different.
Death has such a look of peace.
Surely there is no pain there.
(Would have been 1996, when correctional surgery for
the Chiari deformity didn't remove the pain. By this
time, I was suspecting a spinal cord leak from the pattern
of the pain. But it took until 1999 before I had a doctor
who heard my words. I was even giving nurse quality
reporting in medical terms that they should have
understood.)

MISSING TERRI

I miss the song of Terri
On the stairs.
The lighthearted prancing
Steps of youth.
The rhythmic beat of life filled
With love abundant.
The apartment is not
The same
Without those dancing
Brown eyes,
Jumping curiously form
One thing to another.
Thank you Terri for all the songs,
You put in my heart and mind.

(A neighbor's young daughter so happy and bright.)

THE FORTRESS

Bitter bricks build
On bitter bricks.
Eventually there stands a wall.
This wall to that wall.
A tower makes.
Resentful, bitter feelings
Protecting us from pain.
Surely this great wall
Protects from all.
Then why so lonely
And cold,
So empty and yet full
Of pain?
Where is my God,
My Father?
Has He deserted me too?
The crumbled foundation
Of faith
Work to build a roof.
Trapped in this dark fortress,
Protected from all pain,
Lying in pain.
Nothing can be seen--
No hope, only darkness.
Where is my God,
My Father?
Not understanding
The wall kept God out.
No door, nor window excluded.

God waiting outside patiently
Whispering words of love,
Telling you how to get free.
Loud noises of blame
Screaming from the fortress,
Drowning out the low
And patient voice.
The devil louder still,
Shouting so loud,
God is not heard.
He caused this.
Tears flow inside the fortress,
Cleansing the wounds.
In time, the prisoner
Of the fortress grows quiet.
Now hears God's words.
Scabs fall away
And grows healthy.
The fortress of fear
Crumbles away.
Seeing God and knowing
God, the Father,
Was there all along.
The fortress was an illusion,
But this faith was true.
His God and Father more true.

(Sometimes, we think God has deserted us, but actually, we have shut Him out. With such stout walls to protect us, we can't see God was waiting for us to break down the walls to get to the safety and trust God.)

LONGINGS

Why do I long so ardently
For the time of the long sleep?
My life has been two or three in one.
Too much hardship, pain and sorrow.
Too little rest
Or peace
Or joy.
It continues as such with no relief,
No reprieve.
In short nights, dreams haunt
And taunt,
But in the long sleep, there is nothing
Until, at last our Lord returns.
Then all will be right,
In its proper place.
No longing for sleep,
But long days to fulfill
The wishes of Our Lord.
End these times of bitter strife
With your peace.
Come again my Lord.
Rule over Your people.
Be among us, King.
Let us serve You
And praise You,
Evermore
And evermore.
(This headache thing and my younger son's behavior
issues were really wearing me down. I didn't lose my
faith or I would have committed suicide. Five years of
uncontrolled headaches because it was actually one long,
unrelenting headache before I got some control. Many--
or most-- would have committed suicide if they had
suffered like I had.)

FOUND POEM from an OLD TEXTBOOK

To lie down in my bed
Of the long night's rest,
To pull the dirt up,
Round my ears
And sleep the peaceful
Sleep of sleeps.
A night undisturbed by
Tension, pain, or panic.
This is the sleep l long for,
God don't let it be
Too long in coming.
But, in lieu of that,
Give me the better life
Surrounded by your spirit
And the peace that passes
All understanding.
For there is no peace but,
By You, dear Lord.

(I found this poem in an old textbook on the back
cover. That was not unusual for me to write on anything
that was paper. It was important to just get the feelings
out when they filled me to overflowing.)

HOPE FLOATS

There, seconds after all hope appraised and lost,
Down in depression and despair,
Hope floated up,
Lifted by the life Savior--
God, the Father, Abba, Protector, and
Provider for His children.
Incarnate Lamb, pure sacrifice,
Jesus Christ,
Guide and advocate, Holy Spirit.
All hope, all love, all joy
Comes from You, oh, Lord.
You alone lift us up.

(Most of this depression came from my headache problem. This was just part one of 18 years of suffering from basically one long headache that won't die.)

OCHER STAIN

Lying in the rusty tub,
Gone is pain,
Gone is pain,
Hopeless,
Sadness,
Suffering,
Grief,
Blood going down the drain,
In the tub of ocher stain.

(The headache was a weight that overwhelmed me. I couldn't see any hope because hope because the doctors weren't listening to what I said. I wasn't a hypochondriac. Something real was destroying my life.)

TO DROWN OR NOT TO DROWN?

Face of sadness,
Covered with tears.
Hopeless feelings
Flooding in.
Weights of life pulling down,
Anchor-like,
Descend to the bottom,
Fearful end as bottom-feeder fodder.
But tiny changes cause currents upward.
Life buoyed between anchored bottom
And treading water.
Face the facts,
Breathe when you can or develop gills.
Face the facts,
The salt water around you is not
An ocean or sea.
Face the facts,
The salt water is only tears.
Face the facts,
Live life.
Trust God for your hope.
And for Pete's sake,
Quit crying or
You'll drown.

(Some dark humor seeped into the cracks around the
chronic pain unrelentingly filling so much of my life.)

HOPE

There is always hope in God's way.
Salvation,
Protection,
Resurrection of broken lives.
In all times you are safe,
Loved,
Forgiven.
In His time things will come together.
Patiently,
Patiently,
Hold to hope.
Hope is mature faith.
Hope is faith fulfilled without seeing the results.

(Hope never died in me, but it was a long wait and lot of patience, mostly for medical science to catch up to my need.)

AWAY WITH SADNESS

Throw away sadness.
Do birds show it?
Or flowers grow it?
What good is it?
It stresses,
It depresses,
It distresses,
It drags us down,
Into the ground.
So fertilize it with
All God's blessings.
Grow in the light of the son.
Water with the Holy Spirit.
Grow away from sadness.

(I evaluated and then redirected my attitude to help my ability to cope with this seemingly endless headache problem.)

NIGHT VIGIL FOR MOM

In the morning, too early to see the light,
We wait for the sun to announce a new day.
After a night vigil so tiring,
We hold her hand removed of life.
She had gone silently to her own light,
Moving beyond the present into a place
Of no time restraints or boundaries.
She exists in a healed body now.
Free to move through eternity
Without the constraints of life,
Seeing present, past, and future with
Complete clarity, all at once and
Understanding the difference.
Before, she had been a frightened time traveler,
Confused by a stroke-damaged mind,
Weakened by a failing heart,
Her life and thoughts out of control.
Frustrated by a misunderstood present,
She is saved by the hand of God,
Guided into an eternity of safety and love.

(In 2017, my mom was dying from the complications of a
weakening heart. She had daily bouts of mini-strokes
and mild heart attacks due to clots caused by atrial
fib. My sister and I sat with her as she slowly slipped
away from this life.)

THE WEIGHT OF MY PEARLS

Found are pearls weighty round my neck,
Stringing my life together,
Simultaneously, tearing it apart.
Love unfound, love unfelt,
Acceptance always beyond reach.
Not good enough,
Not good enough,
Whispers winding through my mind.
Blameless, yet, blamed in my brain,
Unaccepted, unacceptable, dejected.
Not good enough,
Not good enough,
No love felt, empty and lonely.
Pearls of wisdom, seeds of depression,
Strung in strangling sadness.

(Today I found the pearls of wisdom that strings my life
together and simultaneously tear my life apart. And
helped the progress of my EMDR.)

DAD

A sad little boy whose father-filled life pushed out self
Grew to a man empty and afraid,
Needy and starved for attention.
A mother too weak to save and protect him,
He married the strength of his life.
In the end, she betrayed him,
Not by will but
By a body frail, sick, and dying,
This man-child being left alone,
Hour by hour, more deserted and desolate.
As her heart weakens,
His heart empties.
He is left again empty and afraid,
His strength goes with her life force.
Fighting for power, he is weakened
And alone in life, vulnerable,
Unprotected.

(My dad grew up in a house with uneven dynamics and
never developed his own inner strength. Mom's death
hit him especial hard. Dad created some difficult
dynamics in my childhood due to his family's
dysfunction.)

DAD's SONG OF LOW SELF-ESTEEM

Assume,
Presume,
Oppose,
Depose,
Rejects,
Objects,
Project,
Deflect,
Self-centered,
Ego-centered,
Negative,
Non-objective,
Narrow,
Farrow,
Opinionated,
Self-hated.

(My Dad has very low self-esteem from an over-bearing
father and a weak, dependent mother.)

TO DAD

You never wanted ME,
Me, the colicky 24/7
Me, the LD
Me, the OCD
Me, the ADHD wiggle-worm
Me, the stubborn
Me, the strong
Me, the smart
Me, the talented
Me, the one who married Denny
Me, the mother of the imperfect
Me, the divorced one
Me, the constant student
Me, the collector of future projects
Me, the ill one with invisible illness
Me, the moody bipolar
Me, that is all I can BE
Me, that are parts of YOU.

(I believe my dad despised me from my colicky entry
into his world, and then despised me even more when
his parts of me confronted him.)

CRAZY KARINA

Thanks to crazy Karina,
You never got free
From your prison.
But you slipped
Me the key,
Left in the bushes
One day.
So I could escape.
And I did
Free from a toxic
Marriage.
Gone to a safe place
Many miles away,
Healing my wounds
Feeding my esteem.
A stronger version
Reborn of the
Dust of my past,
Glowing in a strong
Armor,
Safe in whatever
World I live.

(Karina gave me a copy of Love Gone Wrong by Ann
Jones and Susan Schechter.lt's about control addicts.)

THE PAST

Between the tears,
There was life.
Or did life just
Happen.?
Sometimes pieces of
The past comfort us.
Sometimes pieces of
The past burn us
With pains renewed.

(There has been too much sadness in my life. I survived
by dark humor and tears. I got stronger with each blow
from life.)

THE LAND OF TRUMPMANIA

The troubling times of Trump,
Tearing my country apart.
Tyrannical, white supremist,
Encouraging strife and division,
Lofty from his perch
From a mountain of lies.
Bundles of bills never passed
Cause trauma and division
Even in his own party.
Collusion, delusion,
Glued with more lies.
Wife's cause against bullying
Lives with an overlarge bully.
Distasteful distractor,
Name-calling defamer.
Donald downplaying
His deeds done.
Fake news purveyor
With Trump and friends,
Broadcaster of lies.
Shame of Washington,
Embarrassment of the nation,
Chaos generator,
World imbalancer.
Fear filling the public,
Fearless destroyer of environment.
Swamp drainer
Just to pick his staff.

Trump of idiocracy,
Trump trauma
Continues ad nauseum.

(My life was depressing enough, then we got the
president from hell or idiocracy. And to add to the
picture, he has been accused of multiple cases of sexual
abuse.)

(P.S. This poem may be contaminated so keep it on a
separate page or it can be deleted.)

TEARS FOR MY MOTHER

Born in depression,
During the depression.
Parents of unhappiness,
Independent and angry.
Frustrated with their lives,
Fighting viscous verbal battles,
Controlling and embittered.
Debasing words flung frequently.
Loud and lousy world to come of age.
Married to escape
To a new controlled life.
All is well, if she played her role.
Just go with the flow.
As ages pass, husband sees
Tasks of roles dropped.
Debasing words flung frequently,
Betrayal of duty to her role.
Passive-aggressive, anger expressed.
Loud and lousy world where she died.
Born of depression,
Died of depression,
Worn out and used.
Never appreciated for her true strengths,
So many steps of sadness
Never to satisfy him.
Tears for my mother.

(Mom grew up with many viscous verbal battles, which
made Dad's passive-aggression seem like a safe
haven. As he grew more disabled, he became loud, using
her hearing problems as an excuse. He was actually
expressing his anger about his inability to do what he
wanted. She normalized his abuse over the years and
just took it.)

TO BEATRICE

The song of a child
Is the musical
Notes of laughter.
The dance of a child,
Is happy feet
On the floor.
Oh, to visit simple joy,
In the mind and
Heart of a child.

(I managed to find joy in the depressive loss of my
friend's son and his daughter.)

GOOD-BYE TO DONATA

I once knew a counselor named Donata Moon,
Who proved I was not a loon.
She did EMDR,
Till I saw who I are,
And into my life so soon
Brought a wonderful miracle boon.

(I had gone quite a ways with other therapy choices, but
nothing freed me like EMDR. This limickish ode was my
farewell after completing my therapy and to my
therapist retirement.)

In answer to my poem for her, my clinician, Donata,
responded with this poem ending my EMDR
therapy. Not a poet ordinarily, she had reached beyond
her comfort zone to touch me in like fashion with her
own poem. I close my therapy journal with this poem.

I know a woman so wise,
Who agreed to the "treatment with eyes".
To her true self she awoke,
Saw she'd never really been broke.
Now her limit's as high as the skies!

Old Found Poems: Introduction

Sometimes a significant housecleaning can bring forth forgotten treasures. During a spring housecleaning, I found a box of poems written mostly on scrap-paper. I am adding these

to my second edition of "My Therapy Journal: A Journey of Healing."

Speaking of healing and housecleaning, we all need to do some mental health cleaning by letting go of hurts and anger. My poetry writing helps me clear out and get rid of old issues. Being mindful can also change your focus, so you can let go of the past and not worry about the future. Both of these processes steal energy for the now. It helps to eat clean, periodically use a detox protocol, sleep well, and exercise. A sick body can become so chemically imbalanced it is easier to fall into depression or foul moods. Keep moving on your journey of healing so you can become all the "YOU" that you are meant to be.

CLIMBING OUT

Now as I climb up out of the pit of depression,
I can quit seeing life as so much sordid sadness,
But instead one rich with experience.
Am I melancholy or angry
That I had not allowed antidepressants
Into my life before now? No!
For if I had tried then before
This level of healing won't have occurred,
The pleasures of life would have sunk me
Into a tumultuous trip of guilt.
As if common pleasures were equal
To hedonistic orgies.
My self-esteem so poor.
My right to life without
Punishing behaviors so confused.
And my depth of depression so sense
That I could not cope even with
The calm of normalcy.

(Seeing the good lessons found even in sadness.)

A YEAR OF LOSSES

Losses can mount up
Like a mountainous heap,
Smothering you in pain.
Emptiness, loneliness,
In that one year.
Peter, Gram, Mary,
Carol, and Valerie.
So many gone.

(Five unexpected deaths on top of my decision to get a
divorce.)

CONTROL ADDICT'S POWER

If I rejected control,
I pay.
If I over-rode control,
I pay, joy is taken.
Joy is bought,
So, I may pay.
And what does all this mean,
He wins and I lose.

(My husband was diagnosed as a severe control addict by
our marriage counselor.)

LIFE

The cheerful shouts
And laughter of
Playing children are,
As the song of life,
To me.

(There are always happy moments to catch in life.)

GLORIA

Gloria was a precious dear.
A friend true in all times
Good and bad,
And all the times between.
A tear falls from
Her loss.

(I lost Gloria to cancer far too soon.)

WAIT AND SEE

So many times the knowledge
Of my inadequacy makes me
Long for death.
But, then, a certain knowledge,
Of my future adequacy beckons me
To move toward life.
When I ask what is this thing
Making me too great to end life?
Why must I trust and wait?
Trusting is strengthening,
And in waiting is the touch
Of the Infinite.
We need to have trust to wait.
In waiting is hope and
A strengthening of faith.

(If you too quickly choose suicide you may miss the
experience that will teach you better coping skills and a
sounder support group.)

GO ON FAITH

God doesn't call us
To failure,
But to clarify life.
Sometimes you just
Have to go on faith.

(When life feels like failure, broaden your choices,
experience, and learning.
Failure is a test to learn better ways to succeed.)

A PATH OF LEARNING

Bus
Going down the
Road
With its cheerful load.
Street
Heading for a special treat.
Highway
Of school is a great way.
Avenue
Of daily learning something new.
Lane
Is growing smart is never in vain.
Route
As a day is done and we are out.

(This was mostly a happy word play exercise while the
kids were home schooled.)

OUT OF FOCUS

Knowing God up
Too close to see,
Look for a pattern
And figure it out
Step back and
Really see.

(Sometimes we need to look at a broader picture of our life to recognize where we have met God and His impact on us.)

TENDER MOMENT

How tender was the moment!
How special was that day?
How were we to know A thing could be this way?

(Mindfully appreciate life's blessings whenever they occur.)

PARADOX TRAP

Being loved,
But not believing
In the being
That loves you.

(This can sadly happen in some relationships. This
drains rather than filling us.)

HEALING SCARS

Come and touch my scars
With healing hands
And a gift of grace.
Just touch those scars
Of those of us who have
Been wounded.
Help the lost
To find God.
These scars are a sign
Not seen by others.
How can they help?
Wounds healed by godly
Resurrection.
Our pains taken away
Into the hands of God.

(Some of our wounds are invisible to people, so we must
ask God to show us who can best see and heal us.)

ARCTIC NIGHTSHIFT

At those times when life is dark
And seemingly hopeless,
When no end seems in sight
In the arctic night,
Remember God is there even there,
His presence is known.
In the glory of the Aura borealis
With bright curtains of light.
Shining brightly in the night
In arctic jeweled color.
Direct your eyes upward to hope,
Upward to God.
There, the pathway directs us
Out of despair.
Rainbow drapes of color leading
And promising us,
Even in the deep dark, and lonely
Arctic night shift,
God is there, even there, always.

(Even in the dark of night, God can give us
rainbows. My youngest son inspired this poem with his
picture of the Aura Borealis.)

KINDNESS

You must spend kindness
To buy your happiness,
So, spend kindness
Every chance you get.
Miserly ways leave you
With sadness and
Loneliness.

(This was inspired by a sermon.)

REVELATION IN THE NIGHT

I can't say I should
Have known better.
Experience should have
Taught me something,
But my eyes were closed.
I didn't really want to see.
Life had already showed
Its bleaker side and
I thought that was
Enough for one lifetime,
And I refused to look
At what was happening
For more of the same.

(I was going through trouble that I didn't want to
identify because I'd have to deal with them. But naming
the problems is the first step to fixing them.)

DREAMERS

The world hates dreamers,
They don't fit the mold
Of society.
They pull out and away
From the negative defeatist,
Attitudes which prevail
In the world.

(Inspired by a sermon.)

PURPOSE

Be patient the grass
Eventually becomes milk
Thanks to the work of cows.
God will work
To bring about your purpose
If you will just
Work with Him.
The dream he planted
In you will come to be.

(In a down time a sermon gave me insight in a
purposeful future.)

SUICIDAL THOUGHT

Oh, as I pine for the
Love of death,
Sweet relief from life.
To sleep comforted in
God's arms.
Free from pain, loneliness,
And despair.
To kiss your lips
And be brought
To Your world.
Kiss me now,
Hold tight,
Show me your love.

(Name the pain and your less likely to look at suicide as
an answer. You are also more likely to get help, because
you know kind of help and healing you need.)

IN YOUR THOUGHTS

If you're feeling blue,
Think of when you were two,
And every day,
You just played to play
Every moment of time
Was a nursery rhyme.
Hold to your happy memories
They will give you hope.

(A change in thoughts can shift your attitude.)

GOD IS LOVE

God is love
God loves you.
Love without bounds.
Love as limitless
As eternity.
He gives us His gift
Through Christ,
His beloved son.
Love of the type
That a father has
For his child.

(This is the kind of love that goes everywhere you go.)

DAYS OF SADNESS

In my days of sadness,
I felt as if I was
Sitting in the ashes
With Job.
But at the same time
Were my feelings of
God's great faithfulness.
God gave me a hymn
In my teen years.
"Be Still my Soul."
Through this hymn,
I was repeatedly assured
Of His presence.

When I kept my burdens,
God showed me
He'd take my burdens.
He filled me then
With a song from
Handel's "Messiah",
"Yoke is Easy."
It was His cue
I was carrying too
Much on my shoulders.
It was time to let go.

Now, I have gone through
Divorces, a craniotomy,

Re-entry in college.
He has given me
My new hymn,
"Great Is His Faithfulness."
I feel the truth of it.

(When I hummed or sang these hymns, I felt God's
presence in my life and strength to persevere.)

THE TEAR

Feelings,
Questions,
Understandings
Of life.
All the experience
Of a dying patient
Tied to one's end
With a single tear
Shinning on the verge
Of going down the cheek.

(As an oncology nurse I saw a lot of death, this touched
me very deeply.)

THE HIGH RISE

Three hills of dirt
At our new home site.
Woodchuck's home.
A child's distress over
The home they would lose.
Nature's instinct
Helped them find new digs
Away from harm.

(My young sons worried about the consequences of
leveling the yard for landscaping, because the
woodchucks would lose their earth condo.)

YOUTH RE-VISITED

Teach me to be young.
Somewhere, I've lost my childhood
Teach me to be young
My children are my tutors.
Somewhere, in the muck and mire
Of things I wished to forget,
I lost my childhood.
Too early I needed to grow up
To protect myself,
From a known aggressor.
Clinging to logic
As a protector,
I paid a high price
Of losing my youth.
Teach me the ways
Of the young.

(I repressed much of my childhood because of the
predatory pedophile in the neighborhood. To forget
him, meant losing many of my ordinary childhood
memories.)

FALLING WISDOM

I love the sound of falling leaves
Chattering to each other,
Whispering the secrets of
The colors and smells
Of the seasons,
And describing their saged wisdom
Of advancing time,
The warning of winter's certain coming.
There is a joy in
This riot of colors and
An exhilaration from
The crispness of the air,
That gives us a zest for life,
In exaggeration before
The death of a season.

(I really felt the joy of my favorite season – autumn.)

LIVING WELL

For yesterday is,
But a dream
And tomorrow is
Only a vision,
But today well lived
Makes yesterday a dream
Of happiness and
Every tomorrow
A vision of hope.

(Being mindful of each day.)

ABUSE OF SILENCING

People seeking help
And not getting help
As silence perpetuates.
Growing as with
Sexual, verbal, and physical abuse,
Learned behavior
Of silence in "never tell".
No one had the right
To do that to you,
You're a worthwhile person.
These are acts of violence,
By forcibly holding silence,
This abuse continues.

(Open up, speak up, and get help.)

FOREVER GREEN

As ever the pines are green
In any season,
Frequently, more green
In the harshness of winter.
So is God's love
Ever present,
Stronger through
Our harshest times.

(I have known many rough times in my life, mental and
physical illness. My spirit was frequently stronger when
things were toughest. I knew I couldn't stand alone
without falling I leaned on God.)

DAYS OF GRAY

Days and days of gray
Bleak and nearly black.
All sad inside,
Wishing the sun would
Shine like a giant
Golden globe,
Warm away the bone
Cold from this weather.

(Sometimes I think I must have S.A.D.D. I need some
sun and a doctor to help diagnose.)

STRENGTH TOGETHER

Pray together,
If you have a burden
Weighing you down.
Praying with another
Can act like
Lifting a physical load.
Lifting the burden off
Your shoulders,
Or sharing the load.
Prayer lifts it into
God's hands.
Letting God deal
With excesses of weigh.

(There are some weights too heavy for one person to lift without injury. The same is true for emotional burdens.)

I NEED TO BE NEEDED

Mask with a face,
Sometimes a mirror.
What do you want,
That's what I'll be.
I'm nothing unless
You command it.
In difference is intolerable,
Because that means
I remain nothing.
I need to be something
To do something.
I need to be needed.
Help! I'm breaking up.
I'm falling apart.
How can I be helped?
What of my children?
They must need me?
Thank God!
But they're too little
They can't save me.
Who can help!
Help! Help!
I'm down I'll be
Lost soon! Please!
Need me!

(When you are feeling like this please, please use your
energy to get some help.)

SUMMER DROUGHT

Patchy fields sparse of green,
Looking more like sand dunes.
Birds singing out in mournful tunes.
Tree leaves clapping together in prayer,
Begging the sky for just one drop of water.
Yards of grass dry and golden-brown
While the sky is full of cloud-like down.

(That summer, bare ground was dry and cracked.)

MY SONS

Oh! What sons are these.
One silly and sentimental.
Oh! What a lucky mom.
So cute and hugging,
So handsome and loving.
These my two sons.
Different in coloring
And disposition.
Oh! Lucky mom,
To be given such special gifts
From God above.

(I'm glad my sons were so different I enjoyed some of
the differences very much. But it was hard on my older
son.)

GIFT FROM MY SON

Do you know how much I love you?
Gentle, generous child.
Filled with so much love and joy.
Spilling over into my life.
How much you give me
So much you give me
Without your ever knowing.
So much wisdom in your mind.
You do not take anything for granted.
I have found life a new
Through you.
Bright eyes see the joy
I had forgotten.
Now the joy is in my eyes again,
And I see the world fresh and new.
What insights of knowledge from
Watching you.
Discovering and learning
New understanding unfolds through
Your keen vision.
I love you,
Because of the growth as a person
That happens because of you.
I am great because of what I have
Gained through you.

(There is a symbiosis with mother and child, we grow
because of each other.)

SPECIAL FRIENDS

You saw something in me
That no one else did,
When I was lonely,
You made me feel like I belong
When I was uncertain,
You helped me see things
More clearly.
And you never gave up on me,
Even when I was ready
To give up on myself.
Everything is so much better
For me now,
Because you saw
Something special in me.

(Sometimes a very special friend comes along and brings
the specialness out in you.)

Introduction to New Poems

I am not currently in therapy with a counselor, but I continue to write therapeutic poems. When I find myself ruminating over past events or anxious about future interactions, I know it's time to express my fear or pain in lyrics. The concise format and nature of poems force me to get to the point instead of dribbling on as prose can. Poetry helps me to quickly name the feelings, claim my pain, and deal with it. When the emotions are loosely defined, they can be more easily blame another, making the other person responsible. My feelings and attitudes are my responsibility, which leads to broken relationships stemming from my responses to events. The poetically defined event and reactions are more easily examined and evaluated compared to the real-life events. They are hard to analyze in the "heat of a moment." Poems can be looked at in the cold light of day and judged more clearly.

A poem can describe the incident, then decide on a more appropriate way to deal with the reactions such as:

1. This reaction was on me, so what can I do to course-correct and not use this ineffective response again.
2. Let it go. It was just a "heat of the moment."
3. Avoid this person or similar events.
4. Form new positive relationships that make a healthier self.
5. Consider anger management therapy.

6. Instead of ruminations that can build anger or reopen wounds, try to practice mindfulness to let old issues go.
7. Sign up for training in yoga, tai chi, reiki, meditation, walking, and other activities.
8. Get a hobby such as writing poetry.
9. Get sound sleep without disruption from ruminations.
10. Eat a healthy diet with reduced sugars, no dyes, and other additives. Ask your doctor to check your vitamin, mineral, and electrolyte levels.

This next group of poems is about current issues in my life. Poetry is always there when I need it as long as I have paper and a pencil. Join me on my healing journey with my newest poems.

RELATIONSHIP

Black marks
Under a wedding band,
A scar of a relationship
Deeply beyond repair.
Both parties
Covered with
Scars of life.
Long ago,
Too sore and broken,
To heal together.
The separation was
The best chance.
One was healing
Through years of counsel.
The other passively
Continues in a wounded,
Festering mass
Of discontentment.
Yet open wounds
Invisible to all,
Who would not see.
Tarnish stains
Of black.

(My husband and I both came from dysfunctional
families.)

HIDDEN BUNNIES

Hidden baby bunnies
In grass, not so high.
Three, maybe, five
Small bunnies lie
Near the mailbox
Safe from the mower
Or other maim.
Quietly hiding
So, no one
Would know.
Here and There,
Others hide near
In taller grass tuffs
Throughout the yard.
Watch your step!
And keep the
Bunnies safe.

(This was a happy surprise I found by accident)

AM I?

Disappear
Or nothing?
Actually,
Factually,
What is the
Difference?
Disappear –
No one
Sees you.
Nothing –
You never
Were.
I was something
My life touched
Other lives
I made a
Difference
More than
Once.
Nothing wasn't, isn't,
Never could be,
I have been,
I still am.

(My depression was increasing and I have just before this
poem I started taking Lithium Oratate %mg. daily.)

SUPER HEROES

I know there are
Some who believe
Women's super power
Is bitchery.
That's a term that's
Akin to witchery
Women's true
Super powers are:
Inner strength,
Compassion,
Nurture,
7th and even 8th sense,
Well beyond men's powers.
These super powers
When used
Correctly are a
Marvel to behold.

(Celebrating women's super powers.)

HAIKU

glider high
wings spread wide
free beyond free

(I felt so excited and free on my first glider flight. This
was written in a haiku workshop.)

BROKEN

Misunderstood words.
Broken relationship.
Sense of betrayal.
Bond untied.
End untied.
End without end.
Separated space.
Time lost.
Love eroded.
Pain and anger.
Fills the void.

(This was about my pre-divorce period.)

JOYFUL POTENTIAL

Joy is in
The fulfillment
Of every dream.
Joy is in
The hopefulness
Of every wish.
Joy is in
The faithfulness
Of every heart.
Joy should be in
Every present day
Not just for tomorrow.

(When you can describe an emotion, it is easier to
recognize it in our life.)

ZERO

I want to disappear
By washing the blemish
Away.
The blemish is
My face.
You can't see me.
Lose the weight,
One hundred-thirty.
No! No! more
Down to zero,
No more me!

(Like stresses and days of uncontrolled weather
migraines put me in a deep of depression.)

FINDING JOY

There is no place for joy.
All the spaces are
Filled with stress,
Leading to distress.
Little left to enjoy
Under the weight of strife,
With reduced quality of life.

(Never lose the hope for joy or you won't find it again.)

INAPPROPRIATE

I never knew,
He never told,
Upset and mad.
"I'll never go back,
Never, never back
To that camp,"
He stared at me,
And I wasn't aware
The clear leer.
That was wrong,
Wrong time,
Wrong place.

(My son's experience 30 years later, he told the why of
his childhood comment.)

DOGGY BLUES

I miss my dog,
Gone one lo-o-ong year.
For hugs and belly scratches.
He listened to my woes
And always kept my secrets.
No truer friend,
With unconditional love,
Was my dog.

(A year after my mom died of strokes, my dog also had a series of strokes and died. Two important relationships gone with the same pattern of illness.)

MY LOST MOM

She never really wanted me.
Hate for her mother,
Judged too much like her.
Years of animosity
Friction fraying flaws.
Worked it out too late
Too few years to appreciate
Common grounds and understanding.
Washed away by strokes
The relationship lost
Added brain with memories lost.

(There was usually dysfunction between mom and me,
we only had a short window of togetherness.)

MAKES MIGRAINES MEANINGFUL

Migraines maiming mind to manic maker.
No notion of knowledge not even nonsense.
Can't contain crying or the crankies.
Must make meaningful moments.
Consternation creating crocheted crafts.
Piles produced plenty of product.

(My distraction therapy so I take less pain medication is
crocheting and hand-sewn crafts.)

SORRY TO MY SON

I'm sorry,
I'm sorry,
I'm sorry.
If I would have
Known how much pain
And living in vain,
I brought to you.
I would have
Been childless.
I'm sorry,
I'm so, so sorry!

(My son is in great pain from health problems and
depression. I heard his pain expressed.)

INVISIBLE

Invisible,
In a crowded room.
Invisible,
In my family church.
Invisible,
In my own family.
Invisible,
Speaking or quiet.
Invisible,
Indoors or outdoors.
Invisible,
Skinny or Fat.
Invisible,
Shabby or neat.
Invisible,
When you won't listen to me.
Invisible,
When you don't care for me.
Invisible,
When you have no time for me.
I can be invisible:
Without trying,
Without magic,
Without science,
Without ritual.

(I really hate the feeling of being dismissed, it hurts more
than being hated.)

SECRECTS

For some,
It is more important
To keep the secrets,
Than it is to have
To live with the secrets,
Even when there is abuse.

(About family secrets like: alcoholism, mental health,
and domestic abuse.)

MY EVERYWHERE THERAPIST

I'm leaning on my Lord
When times are tough.
Living with thoughts
And feelings that
Get really rough,
I have someone to Talk to.
When no one else
Wants to listen,
I'm leaning on my Lord.
No need for an appointment,
No special day or time,
I just talk wherever I am.
Or listen for His quiet and calm.
To settle my qualms.
I'm leaning on my Lord.

(Sometimes, you just need to talk it out, that sorts out a
lot of problems,)

LYING LEADER

You will know
I found you
Lying out loud,
In front of a crowd,
With no sense
Of shame.
But plenty of blame.
Do you see the
Problems of,
Feeding this information
To so many people
Or are they sheeple?
They believe
While you deceive?
How long will
They be still?
(You know who.)
Busyness
Sometimes we get so
Caught up in the
Busyness of life we
Forget to live life.

(I don't feel worthy unless I'm producing some kind of
crafts.)

I NEED A GOOD CRY

Sometimes I feel like
I need a good cry
To lubricate my emotions.
I have my special movie,
A sappy-sad one.
I always cry at the end.
A never-fail trigger
The right sappy-sad,
To make the tears flow,
"Affair to Remember."
My old friend,
Who lets me cry
Without judgement,
Wound cleansing tears.
Flow a little or a lot,
But always just right.

(Crying is like the valve on a pressure cooker, it takes away the extra stress and pressure. Very cleaning and healing. I knew someone who cried in the shower so no one else knew.)

BIPOLAR ME

Illusion, delusion,
Mood swings and more.
Bipolar bounces
Down in the dumpster
Deep in depression,
Fly in the sky
High as a kite.
Where will you
Mind and body
Go today?
Climb on the rooftop?
Busy projects piled
Mountain peak tall,
Then balled up in bed
Can't get started.
Life is a roller coaster,
Going in continuous circles.
Wishes for one
Middle mood and
Forward movement.

(Usually I stay in one mood for days or weeks, but if I'm
extra stressed I cycle more frequently.)

PRODUCT PILES

Constant action
With production,
Objects from work
Signify worth.
Onward pushing,
More to prove
Personal worth,
Working, working,
Always working.
Increasingly active,
Worth is production
Measured in numbers.
Zero is zero worth.
Piles of products,
Drives out the
Worthlessness.
More and more product
Driving ever forward,
The proof of worth
Measured in Plentiful piles.

(I really have problem feeling worthy if I don't have
products of work.)

EMPTY WITHOUT YOU

Empty without you,
I feel a cold sickness
In my stomach.
A hurting emptiness,
In my heart,
When I think of
Life without you.
You saved my life,
When I knew you
Were the life
Within me.
I cannot bear,
The thought of
Life without you,
Live long,
Live strong.

(I was considering suicide when I realized I was
pregnant. Again, sadness has filled me with suicidal
ends, that same child gives me a will to live.)

THE POWER OF POETRY

A defuser of pain,
My poetry became
A defuser of pain
From the emotional bane
Overwhelming again.

Feelings locked in my core
Strongly erode from every pore,
Corrosive lye of life,
Carrying me through my strife.
Soul eating,
Flesh eating.
With feelings repression,
Grows deeper depression.
Pushed down
By a frown,
Push it out
With a great shout.
Written words
Moves outwards.
Diluted with a few tears,
Lessens so many fears.
A defuser of pain,
My poetry became
A defuser of pain,
From the emotion's bane
On my mind again.

(I work through a lot of emotional pain with the power
of poetry with no one to judge me or tell my secrets. I
share now to help people get past their emotional
repression. Repression like a physical wound can go
systemic if untreated. Does your emotional pain make
your body hurt and feel ill? Let it out! Write it!)

?WHY?

Why???
Why exist?
Why does anything exist?
Any being?
Any place?
Any time?
Why the universe?
Why any space filled?
Why animate or inanimate?
Why? Is this a cosmic joke?
It's not funny!

(My son's question of why is there any existence?!?)

A CHICKEN'S COUNSEL

"Why did the chicken cross the road?"
"To get to the 'other side.'"
It's a suicide riddle.
So, cross the road
Only to get counsel.
Don't be a chicken.
When support is available for,
A better life.
The 'other side' will
Wait a few years.
You are worthy of life!
Live strong!
Live long!

(There is always another choice, but its hard to see them when your depressed. Counselors can help you see expanded choices. Please get help, you are special.)

THE EMPTY ZONE

Always rejected.
Rarely protected.
He was clinging.
Wished possessing.
Lost in the great empty.
Nothing inside, but empty.
Desperate for filling,
No one was willing.
Wanted to talk to her.
Decided to stalk her.
Feeling unwanted,
Deeper rejected,
Became more obsessive,
Clinging possessive.
Smothered wife,
In emotional life.
On his heart tread,
All of him dead.
Left all alone,
In the empty zone.

(This was my relationship with a man from a
dysfunctional family from dating to divorce.)

AFTERMATH OF AN ARGUMENT

"How much do you hate me?"
"Really?"
"How much do you hate?"
"Why, didn't you ask me,
What I actually said, instead of this
Misunderstood message?"
I lost my son due to my tongue!
"Why do you hate me?"
It's already too hard,
For me to love me!

(I argued with my youngest son and he left before, I
finished my sentence. Eight years ago. My heart is still
broken between the tears.)

47 ASPIRINS

One by one,
Then a few,
Done by done,
Set my curfew.
No pain,
No distain,
No loss,
In this loss.
Silent in night,
Gone with light.
One by one,
Then a few,
Done by done,
My own curfew.

(I was depressed and stressed by my fiancé who I didn't
want to marry. He was pushing me to move in with him
after I graduated. No way! If I was dead, I won't have
to! It was nearly a suicide. There were more choices I
just didn't see them.)

TODAY AT A GLANCE

Today at a glance,
Leftovers of the old society.
The dregs uniting in tribes,
To find safety within,
From a sick planet
And a sicker society.
Lack of empathy,
With closed feelings.
Limited communication
With decline in connection,
Family units broken,
Held together with soluble glue.
Covered in tears
And floods of fears.
Repressed remembrance
Generalized and gone systemic.
Remnants left
Filled with remorse,
Frozen in time,
Silence swaddles
Unhealable wounds.
Rejecting compassion
And comfort,
Society stays sick.

(These are thoughts about my personal understanding of
"The Leftovers", life, and society currently at large.)

TRUMP – McCONNELL VANITY WALL

Trump's vanity project,
The Trump – McConnell Wall
Held up so long,
Trump set in motion
The Trump – McConnell Shutdown.
Because Trump won't accept
A lower Trump – McConnell Wall
Funds which Trump
Promised Mexico would pay,
Not America.
But what it will become
Is mafia-like protection money
From Mexico (the Trump trade deal)
OR
The Trump – McConnell People Tax
To pay for the Trump Vanity Wall.
The concrete or steel wall will corrode,
And filling tunnels will cost
Huge amounts to repair.
All along it is known
Electronics and more staff
Is much more effective
And much less costly.

(To date only about five miles of new wall has been build
and some of that is already falling apart due to poor
planning and supplies. People easily climb over the
fence. There have been properties confiscated from
private property. Champaign promises not fulfilled.)

CONDESCENSION

When you look at me
What do you see?
Do you see the depression,
From memory repression?
Do you see
The psych-physical scars on me?
Do you see a dysfunctional brain,
Which caused 18 years of pain?
Do you see the clinical loneliness
From broken relationlessness?
What would you see
In a mirror instead of me?
What is your conception of my vision,
It sure looks like condescension.
You don't see me,
Just your opinion of me,
Tainted with bias.
"The poor" us.
Lined up in heat or freeze,
Food for those pathic ones,
That life has been cruel.
Dismissal or condescension,
Because we missed our life vision.
Would you accept that look
From your safe, comfy nook?

(Even people who are doing kindnesses can show
condescension with presumed lesser people.)

WRONG

"Relationships" are at the
Root of my wrongs:
Wrong people,
Wrong time,
Wrong type of relationship,
Acquaintances that never
Should have been friends.
"Friends" that just use.
Healthy boundaries
Misunderstood,
Lack of respect
For my rights,
One-sided rights and wants
More for them.

(I seem to have too many of the wrong people in my life
at any given time. Relationships "blood" or "friend" are
just not a good fit.)

BELOW THE DOME

The depth of
My depression,
Will soon drown me
Sinking below
The air of life,
The pressure of life.
Pressing me downward
There is more doubt,
Than hope.
Only doom
Below the dome
Of depression.
I'll search for life
In the dawn of new life.

(I was feeling smashed by the weight of depression from
life out of my control. I increased my lithium oratate
from 5mg. daily to twice a day.)

FILLING SPACE

I've lived beyond
The time I wished
Sad years last longer.
Happy years go too fast,
Go on to time filled:
With fun,
With success,
Something worthy of
Filling a life,
Worthy of the space
I took up,
On a crowded planet.

(Since I was a teenager, I felt unworthy of taking up
space on an over-full planet.)

ENDLESS

I am like Sisyphus,
Pushing my life load
Always up steep hills.
Tired of the work,
More from the work,
So much work,
Lacking gain or salary.
Why do I continue the effort?
Exhaustion leads to:
Mindless effort,
Purposeless effort,
Doing for the sake of doing.
The load of life
Always rolls downhill.
Never reaching the top.

(I feel like I'm just going through the motions of life
without making any actual progress.)

WHY IS EXISTENCE?

Why life?
Why exist?
Why ever?
What purpose is life?
What purpose is existence?
Why does anything ever exist?
Why?!?
Why fight for life?
Why fight for existence?
Without purpose?
With suffering?
With strife?
With struggle?
With stress? Why?!?

(A revisit of the question of why does anything exist and
for what purpose.)

NEVER

Never fell in love.
Had three crushes,
Left my heart
Empty and yearning.
For emptiness
To be fullness.
Hope is as empty
As my heart.
Lost relationships
That never happened.
How can you heal,
From a wound
Never been cut,
Never all together?

(At my age and no love of my life or soulmate,)

DISMISS

You may
Dismiss me:
By race,
By religion,
By sex,
By size,
By age,
By talent,
By job,
By education,
By experience,
But you will never
Be able to
Dismiss my personhood.

(We have a dismissive society that leaves too many
people unwanted and alienated.)

PURE EVIL

When pure evil and corruption arrives,
Soul-less and empty,
We must,
Empty their bloodless soul
As empty as their soul space.
Destruction of evil
So, it spreads no more.
Transfuse them with purified blood
We need a return
To purer spirits
Creative and positive.
Stop the corruption
Of the world,
Filled with death
And shrouds.
Corruption sucking out life
Must end.
Balance of homeostasis
Must return
Metamorphosis to clean and good.

(There seems to be way too many soup-less people filled
with corruptive evil in society,)

BEAUTY ON THE BEACH

I saw on a barren beach
One thing of beauty,
A bright and sunny face.
Boldly, strongly,
Calling for your attention,
To the strength of
Her presence.
Suddenly, that beach was full:
Of her beauty,
Of her potential.
And I knew my
Life was fuller,
From her existence
In my world.

I was awed by this simple beauty of friend's
granddaughter on an empty beach, Her presence
commanded my attention.)

BUTTERFLY GIRL

Two butterflies,
One for each hand.
Beautiful picture
So close to nature,
Awed by their beauty
Pure and simple.

(Children are so pure and innocent. They are awed by
nature, making an awesome image.)

CORONAVIRUS

Life on hold,
In the house we're told,
Closed up we stay,
So, we don't go away.

Keep us safe,
In our place.
Keep us safe,
At a slower pace.

Better to stay healthy,
Than push to be wealthy.
Isolation is the best med,
Better than being dead.

(Even when I'm not in professional therapy, I write
poetry to vent or praise and respect my blessings,)

DON'T FEED THE GREED

Crack down on greedy corporate bai-outs,
The execs suck up the money for buy-backs,
While, mom and pop shops need the help,
And regular people are drowning in debt.
Full of fear of losing their home,
The covid-19 jobless working poor
Need help with money for:
Food, home, and much more.
Get the homeless into homes
So, they can be safe in isolation too,
Helping the poorest of the poor,
Helps saving all American people.
With enough supplies to test and care.
America needs:
Tests and testing equipment,
Isolation gear – masks, gowns, gloves,
C-paps, respirators,
Rooms and more beds.
Put the money where we need it,
Don't feed the greedy, they'll just eat it or
Hoard it.

(This was written on 3/22/2020 we still need some
equipment and will continue to need supplies, because
we are not all doing what we need to do to stop this
pandemic. Our selfishness to do what we want will keep
COVID alive for years. Now, 200,000 dead and
counting.)

COVID-19 PANDEMIC

Help delayed by a month or more
And ineptitude in leadership.
Trump lied and people died.
The coughing, grabbing like a claw,
Strangles out the air,
Emptying lungs of oxygen
With Covid-19
After you burn up with
A fever of 101 degrees and much more.
Muscle aches and headaches,
Dry, hacking cough so severe
A rib nearly breaks.
In a body that already aches.
Where were the tests to
Get help sooner?
How many respirators
Can be made in a day?
How many more hospital rooms?
How many graves?
Trump lied! People died!

(As a retired nurse I know speedy action saves lives and
so does high quality leadership.)

HIS SLAVE

Something lost in his brother's view
Was seen by me.
His brother only saw the work,
He'd do with proficient expertise.
His brother was his slave,
For all unwanted tasks.
Never allowed to question
Without receiving verbal abuse.
"Shut up and do it!"
Was the message.
The older one less capable
Ashamed to admit it,
Too inept or maybe lazy to do the job.
The younger exhausted from all his jobs
Too weary to argue his rights.
This from a man, who decries
The slavery of his family's past.
He's made his brother –
His personal slave,
Verbally abusing him never
Allowing protests or asking to share tasks.

(My dear friend, who I love as a son is abused by
unshared work loads and verbal abuse. Sometimes by
physical abuse. If I protest this behavior, he gets more
abuse.)

DEARLY

To the one I love so dearly,
I know your worth,
I feel your pain.
I see the many tasks you do,
Some done before I ask,
Done more proficiently than another.
I know in your quiet ways,
There is a depth of knowledge
Filled by your love of learning.
You have grown
And matured,
Capable and strong.
While another, stands still,
A perpetual child.
You, instead are a man
Carrying all the burden of two.
I hug you in my heart,
Even when you are not near,
Because, you are so very dear.

(I know two brothers, one outspoken and brash. The
other quiet and very special. I feel so blessed having the
latter in my life. Frustrated by the other.)

A THANK YOU

A thank you,
Is nice
When you
Do a lot,
That another
Will not.
Just a thank you.
Especially,
With a list
Of all you
Actually did
Is better yet!

(When someone just expects you to do it all and they do
any of the job, it really hurts when it is not respected for
the "all" that is in your expected list.)

STROKES

I do more
When I get
Strokes
Otherwise,
I won't try.

(some people don't have mutual respect without an
abundance of strokes. Mutual respect needs a sharing
mindset,)

UNDERSTANDING THE NOW

Magically, magically.
Time passes by,
Sometimes too fast,
Sometimes too slow.
But, somehow
The storyline
Is too hard
To understand
Unless you see
It as history.
How long will
We need
To understand
This present story?
Handling the needs
Of supplies and action
During a pandemic.

(This crisis is so complex and poorly handled it will take
years to dissect the truth.)

BERNIE BROS

Progressive purists
Fighting "the lost cause",
Lock-stepping and uniformed in
The glow of purity.
They don't get Bernie has lost.
If he is so prefect and powerful,
Why didn't he get universal Healthcare
While he was a senator?
OOP! He doesn't play nice with others,
He never formed a coalition.
A like minded group will work better for a cause.
There is no such thing as purity or perfect,
With a group of one hundred,
With a hundred different ideals.
One pure, perfect can't happen with millions
Of Americans.
Purity and perfection is an unrealistic fantasy,
Eutopia in dystopia, never to be achieved.
Welcome to reality.

(You just have to work together for the closest to the
best and realistically that may have to happen in steps.)

UNSTUPIFYING OF AMERICA

How do you get away from the lies?
Here is a pleasant surprise,
Watching multiple news networks
Gets different points of view,
Watching only one network
Will only confirm your bias.
Truth is always beyond your opinion,
Check more sources can vet information
Through fact checking, because facts are truth.
Opinions are slippery and changing,
Truth is only in facts.

(Without research, you can be fooled into clinging to lies
or opinions which changes by person or time. Facts
don't change, like it or not.)

HIAKU

like a dragon
stomping through the sky
rolls and roars
the thunder

wind blown tress
chatter about
spring hopes

GROWN-UP ADULTS

Growing less mature
As we move forward in time,
No wonder so few
Can handle the life
We are living now.
Some as oppositional,
Petulant, angsty as teenagers.
Grown-ups, seek the truth
And act accordingly.
Not liking the facts
And believing the lies,
Won't make it go away
Or make it better.

(There are currently too many so-called adults who need to
grow up so we all can better face and fight the present crisis.)

APRIL TORNADO

Stealthy monster hidden
In the fiercesome sounds,
Winds rattling tree branches,
Large hail pelting windows.
Lightening teasing glimpses
Of broken trees falling,
Then the radar comma
Names the threat,
Darkness hides a tornado.
Moving from town to town,
Trashing buildings,
Power lines, and trees
Only the morning light,
Confirms
What caused the damage.

(I watched the weatherman explain the danger as I
waited for news about a family member in the ER for a
health crisis.)

HIAKU

snow snow
on the ground
april surprise
one day now two

(It ended up that there was 4 snow days in April and 3 in
May.)

spring buds
on the tree
are apples by fall

winter's potatoes
buried in dirt
grow tater families
by fall

(Anticipation of a fall harvest, not a good year for apples,
there were only 9.)

GETTING UP

Resisting morning action
Getting up was so hard
To do in the 90's,
Brain crushing pain
From low spinal pressure
Caused by a leak.
2010 on was a
Dizzying daunting effort,
From low blood pressure
And low pulse,
Both caused a war
In my head
To want to get up
And start to get moving.

(Life is a challenge with health problems.)

AGAIN!

Sakes! It's snakes
Present stressors
Triggered past times
Flashback nightmare
Of my bed,
Filled with snakes.
Wiggling, wriggling,
Under the blanket.
Covering the top, too!
Waving the blanket,
Shaking and tossing,
But none of them
Will leave.
Struck in my bed
With squirming snakes.
Only awakening
Made them leave.

(Childhood nightmares returned with the high stress
of several issues happening within weeks.)

GROWING FEAR OF NUMBERS

It's happening more
Pulses of 120, 160,
Then one night
Pulse to 177,
Then on to 191.
"Call 911, now",
Chest tight,
Pickily and numb,
Left arm.
Tight chest tighter,
Pulseox 88%.,
"I can't catch my breath.'
"My son so pale,
Panic or organic?"
39-year-old heart,
Not knowing a cause
Growing fear
On to the ER.
Then a tornado blew
Through by 11 PM.

(Fear was compounded by the numbers, sick and/or
dying from COVID-19.)

CIRCLE OF NOISE

Persistent yelling, screaming,
Were her parents
When present together.
Then her newborn,
Twenty-four- seven.
Persistent yelling, screaming.
Colicky child constant,
Months and months
Goes on,
Triggered memories
Of her childhood.
Later, baby grandson,
Persisent, yelling, screaming
Hours and hours.
While, she was caring,
For my son
While, I was at work.
Triggered memories,
Of life on high volume,
Circle of noise.

(Sorry Mom, I didn't realize at the time I was triggering
your childhood issues.
Example of Random Access Memory (RAM).)

LOST SKILLS

People whining
And wailing
Stuck in their homes
With nothing to do.
Let us out!
Let us out!
Happy am I
So many projects
Just waiting in line
So, time is mine:
Afghans,
Corona masks,
Tote bags,
Poems and essays,
Plus, stories to write.
Why do others
Whine and wail?
Can't they self- entertain
Anymore?

(People who complain about no time for household
projects, now complain about being at home?!? Really?!?

SELFISH AND CRUEL

Don't trash my sons, Dad
First, the youngest,
Hyperactive and impulsive.
"Can't he behave?"
"He's always in something!"
"He's too busy."
On and on,
About two decades.
Then, it was the elder,
Who called his gramp out
For sass and cruel
Talk to his grandma.
This son was protecting
His grandma.
Years later when
She wanted to help Him,
With her arm in a sling,
"No need to help me."
He was again protecting
His grandma.
Then his gramp sullied his
Grandson's name again.
Never to do right to this day.
"Where does he go so much?
I though he was sick?"
After a trip to ER,
For a pulse way too high,
"What does he have

To be anxious about?"
"How hateful and critical
Can you get, Dad?"
"Get out of your own shell, Dad!
You only care if it's about You."

(So selfish, he can't see other people have health issues,
you're not alone. You, Dad, caused your own current
health issues, but grandson has several autoimmune
diseases not of his own doing. Everyone has times of
suffering. Try some compassion. There is a big world of
people beyond you.)

HOSTA

Hostile about his Hosta.
Horticulturally productive,
Having planted them all over.
Handling the buds,
Hah! What a sound,
Happy kid noises
Hosta bud, POP's!
Hurry he's angry
Hands shouldn't touch!
Hosta buds ever.
Hateful stares follow us.
Hie away and Hide!

(The spring renewal of Hosta, renewed a memory of the molesting neighbor's hostile attitude about his Hosta and our rebellious popping of the buds. He touched us, so we touched his Hosta buds.)

EMOTIONAL CONTROL

Emotionally repressed
To the point of
Being sterile,
Continually depressed
Without strife.
Nothingness is stress,
Waiting for the distress,
Fear filling the unknown
Uncontrollable to bemoan.
The price of control
Is a low level of spirit.

(Suppressing emotions wears as much as worries of fears
from the unknown.)

MISSING THE CALL

If I had given in
To the call of death,
I won't have lived
A life of chronic depression.
I won't have gone
Through others strife.
But I'd have missed
The special joys of life.
I won't have grown
Stronger and
Been the me I am now
Missing the call
Saved my life.

(Looking back on my life it was rough and good, death
would have taken good from my future.)

THE ARGUMENT

Started as polite conversation
Then I realized . . .
What he was saying,
"I'm not cleaning cat litter,
So, I'm not washing my clothes here."
Following him out the door
And down the driveway,
I felt the heat raise.
Then he spewed out
His anger about . . .
The ADHD meds,
The response to past behaviors,
The mismanagement of his
Legal issues.
I stood defending myself from,
His venom and
Side-kicked his shoe.
In minutes,
He was leaving and
I didn't get to
Finish my comments.
Filling in the blanks
Of what I never said,
Then he lied about,
What I said and did.
He had an excuse
To never come home.

(I had a deal with him, clean the cat litter from his cats
for using my laundry. He had left the cats at my
house. My older son and I had health problems and it
was very difficult for us to care for the cats.)

MAGNETIC REPULSION

Like magnets whose poles repulsed
I felt the distance expand
Between my mom and myself
Trigging her past
With her own mother
Hurtful, hollow relationships
With substance nurture
But no healing for emotional needs
Together with an abyss between us.

(Triggered by Darrell Hammond's "Cracked Up"
special.)

LITTLE RED RIDING HOOD

Had more than wolves to fear
It isn't always the stranger danger
That is the most unsafe,
It isn't always the monster –
Under the bed
Or in the closet
The real danger can be,
Living in plain sight –
A friend,
A neighbor,
A relative,
Or someone else . . .
Who you thought was safe
And others believed were safe.

(My mom gave us the "no candy from strangers" talk a
few years too late.
My sister and I had already been introduced to danger
and he was no stranger. He was the kindly grandpa-type
neighbor.)

PTSD – COVID-19

Who are going to be there,
To save the survivors of
COVID-19 with ARDS.
While in drug induced coma
Their minds filled with
Horrific hallucinations.
Come back after
A fight for life
Overwhelmed with PTSD,
Counselors unite and encircle them
With healing and hope.
Friends and family
Help fulfill their needs
For complete healing.
Save the survivors
From the emotional wounds,
Cut the post-COVID losses
Don't Make America Grave Again.

(There is more to just survivor's of COVID and the
physical healing, there is also the mental damage and
increased chances of suicide.

DAILY MOURNING

America in mourning,
America every morning.
More deaths daily
Raising numbers
Reaching to the sky in bodies.
Still too few tests,
Still too few masks,
Still too few gloves,
Still too few protections,
Still too few pieces of equipment,
Raising cases of positive,
Raising fear of death.
Will there be room
Beyond the ICU,
For so many graves.
Will there be too few
Alive to mourn.
America in Mourning.

(Trump ran in 2016 with the slogan, "Make America Great Again", it looks more like make America grave again and again, with 200,000 + and counting.)

UNMASKED TRUTH

All the president's
Men and women,
Falling sick from COVID-19.
Unmasked he shows
No compassion.
Unmasked he shows
No understanding,
Unmasked his zealots,
Still don't see
His true face,
A malignant narcissus
With present hedonism.
More will fall due to
His selfish desires
Open the country,
So, he will look great.
What is the problem
With a few sick
Or dead?
He's alive and safe,
What else matters,
Seems to be his message?!?

(With my nursing background, this inept behavior,
frustrates my nursey senses to heal people and prevent
disease.)

HIDDEN BEAUTY

There was a window in time,
When I had some beauty,
But I ate my way
Through depression
And life stress'n.
Fat hid my beauty
Until it was lost
In rolls and bulges.
When I lost the weight
The beauty was lost
In creases and crepe
Just a dried-up prune.
Luckily, my heart shines
With beauty.

(Let your true beauty shine with a compassionate, loving
heart. Your greatest beauty is deeper than skin.)

NON – SYBIL

Not like Sybil,
No other people to be,
No one to save me,
No one to comfort me,
No one to scape goat,
Or lay the blame on
Other than me.
I coped and went
On alone for
Too many years.
Memories pushed down
So, I couldn't see,
Even me.

(Fortunately, when the memories forced their way up to my thinking brain, I thought, I need to fond a counselor and make an appointment. Get help if you need it, too.)

PERSONHOOD DISMISSED

My personhood on the line.
My very existence questioned,
Less than a wallflower.
I am nothing,
Less than nothing –
So, nothing?
I am empty of life.
Too much a non – person
No one else knows my presence.
No one addresses my name
I am dismissed of all
Personhood or presence.
In my world,
Never to be seen.

(In public places, people look through and passed
everyone never seeing others personhood.)

"MASKED VOICES"

Masked language
Muffled words
Muted sounds
Mumbled voices
Muzzled opinions
Mangled messages
Message lost
Misunderstood words
Meaning void
Mashed, mixed and muddled
Modified comment
Meddled words
Misjudged meanings
Misconceived statement
Minimized message
Mendacity, mephitic words.

(Even when there are no masks on our faces, people
mask the meaning of their messages to hide their
prejudices from self and others.)

THE TEAR

The tear that told,
What she really felt.
It wasn't funny,
Not a joke.
It was nasty.
Hurt held in like a
Pin pushed in just for pain.
Layers of years
Scars deeper than skin.
One time too many,
Rude words spoken.
I witnessed the pain,
Glistening bright
In a single tear
Sliding down
A sloping cheek.

(My dad thought he was cute with his sassy remarks, but one day I saw how hurtful his remarks were when a tear ran down his mother's cheek.)

THE PROTOCOL

Four years of foreplay
Spoils all future foreplay
Forever more.
Pedophiles' protocol
Years and years of grooming,
For the future coitus
Is that the way,
For years and years,
Did he groom his daughter?
Then, for years and years
Of coitus,
Filled her uterus with
His daughter-granddaughter.

(After my molester was caught, we found he had been an
    incestuous father and got his daughter pregnant.)

ASEXUAL

So many sexual definers
Exist in our vocabulary.
This is the one I choose,
Asexual.
Too many years
Of a pedophile's predatory foreplay
Now foreplay triggers –
Shutdown,
Not joy to enjoy.
For me, I choose,
Asexual.
No, thank you,
For any sex.

(Molestation can change the dynamics of relationships
on many layers,)

NO! AUTO MOBILE

No car for you.
No place, but here.
Controlled by no mobility,
Stay at Home,
So, you won't roam free
Left alone at Home
Punishing control
NO! car to GO!
NO! to visit family.
NO! to friends.
NO! to go shopping.
NO! to go to doctors.
Yes, to go to work.
Yes, to get a paycheck.
Yes, to pay all the bills.
Controlled by NO auto mobility
NO cage needed,
Without a car.
His Control.

(I left one night after work to my parents' NOT to my
home after he embarrassed me with put-downs. He
reaped up the transmission of a car I worked three years
to get. Control-addicts mode in full gear. No car for you,
you'll never leave me again.)

SABRINA'S SMILE

Sabrina's smile
Makes the whole world
Shine a lot Brighter.
Sunshine or moonshine,
Stars or none,
No light in the sky.
Sabrina's smile
Brightens any day!
You make my
World brighter!

(I saw a Facebook picture of a family friend's
granddaughter.)

FOOD PHOBIC

When food becomes poison
In the mind,
Don't force more in
Even with weight loss.
"Baby Steps" into food,
One new choice per day.
Too fast overwhelms
From forced food
On a Broken body.
Fighting a brain
That feels fearful
And under attack.
Anxiety feeds anxiety.
Go gently,
Calming the fears
Comforting the soul.
Moving to heal the
Fear of food.

(My anxiety about poor leadership during COVID-19
plague got so over-whelming and I couldn't tamp it down
any longer. It turned into food phobia.)

COVID CRISIS

COVID negative
Body still suffers,
Body on fire,
From hyper-immune system.
Everything is enemy,
Food and pills allergens,
Increase in numbers.
A world of danger,
Incompetent leader lost control.
Hyper-vigilant body,
In flight, fight, and freeze mode.
Flight with tachy pulse,
Fight builds to chest pain and tight,
Freeze blood pressure drops,
COVID body crisis.
Fluctuates between modes.
Body confused by mode shifts,
Bodily imbalanced, out of control.
Survival remedy needs
Stability and safety.

(Five trips to the emergency room with many tests begs
the question, was this cardiomyopathy?)

WHAT IS HAPPENING?

Food eaten,
Chest grows tight,
Then the throat
Is it an allergy?
Ambulance to ER
Treated as allergy?
No, it's pulmonary emboli,
Chest x-ray and CAT scan,
Blood work,
Electrolytes,
Cardiac enzymes, and more.
Cardio-sonogram, and
Cardiac catheter.
Three events to ER.
It's anxiety attacks,
Tests show it never
Was a food allergy.
Maybe, fragrance with
Respiratory reaction.
Heart is fine,
Vital signs waiver
Pulse is sky high and
Blood pressure is basement deep.
Heal the broken body
Wounded by anxiety.

(Hypervigilance over triggered an inflamed vagus nerve
. "Anxious Staticus", became the norm for over a
month. Allergy tests calms my nerves, so I could relax.)

BEATEN DOWN by CHAOS

Beaten down by chaos,
My body worn and
Bruised by emotional damage.
Inept, selfish choices
By "so-called" leadership
Hit like punching fists
Tearing into my psyche,
Wounding to the core,
No more fight left in me
To defend from this fiend,
My body attacks self.
Beaten down by,
Current circumstances,
Self-punished by my
Inability to defend self.
Starving my body
With food phobia
In a prison of chaos
Located in COVID country.

(My anxiety about things I couldn't control turned into
control of food intake. This is not safe.)

ANXIETY

Anxiety pouring over me
Like a corrosive chemical,
Burning through my protective systems.
Self-defenses turn into,
Self attacking self,
Anxiety's destructive forces
Breaking my body down.
Flight, fight, or freeze:
Turned self-destructive
False-allergic responses
Food no longer feeds
Draining, straining,
Life-forces leaks out,
Sapping strength,
And energy out,
Weaking, weightless
Body wanes and fades.

(I went from 115 pounds to 103 in just 3 weeks. I was
controlling actions, but not my health. It didn't control
the world around me.)

The DON of DEATH'S DOMAIN

Barely, fairly good enough,
How he's handled our care.
He hardly has a
Concept of compassion or care
With so many sick,
And he himself still sick,
Stuffed full of sciences solutions.
Going out grabbing large groups
In super spreader sessions,
Sizzling and seizing
With raging wrath,
This person passing on pure lies
Putting polarized populations,
In jeopardy through unjust poor judgement.
Is it thoroughly thoughtless
Or a maniacal masterplan
Of pure and perfect punishment?
From a dishonest dignitary
To a disgusting disloyal people.
Hugs, kisses, and closely confined crowds
Inoculated masses incubating illness,
Spread in states the special sickness.
This man leaving his mark
Disastrously destroying lives and families
Demarked throughout distant history
In his domain as the Don of Death.

(Even as he knows he is still sick he spreads   COVID and misinformation to a manipulated population.

LOVE ME AS I AM

He never knew,
As he early knew,
Nothing about it,
Yet claims
Knowledge of
Everything about,
Every topic and issue.
This monstrous moron,
Of stable genius
Haphazardly manipulates,
Truth to suit his need,
At stage center
At all times,
To be seen and heard,
Spewing word soup
And salad
Of inarticulate
Almost sentences,
Of thoughtless thoughts.
As a grifting slight
Of hand,
Off-handedly
Conspiracies spread,
Molding many minds
That no one else
Is worthy.
Just love me,
Follow me fans

To the ends of the earth
And life,
Just love ME!
He whined pathetically.

(This needy and never to be filled up person desperately
demands love as he lies)

SELFISH SHORTSIGHTEDNESS

In a selfish need to obstruct
An option to safely vote.
The post office system
Was put in suspended
Animation,
Reducing staff,
Reducing funds,
Never recognizing others' needs
Fulfilled by postal delivery.
Senior and disabled persons',
Prescription medications
Vitamins and other supplements
Medical supplies and more,
Some even their food.
Unable to easily shop in stores.
Online and phone-in-orders,
Parcels come by
Postal delivery often.
For those without computers
Correspondence courses and classes.
Maintaining communications
With families and friends.
There are so many
Ways the U.S. postal services
Keep us connected,
And supplied with our needs.
The selfish one so short-sighted
Has deprived us from more
Than a safe way to vote.

(Someone is afraid of losing, but we the people have lost
more.)

PEDOPHILE'S PARADISE

Living on a private street
Loaded with kids,
Boys and girls,
Divided between five houses.
More who come from
Other nearby streets,
For sports and other play.
Babies, toddlers, and preteens,
There is also a man.
Not a stranger with candy,
We were the candy
In a store full of merchandise.
I spent my childhood
In a pedophile's paradise.
Until someone caught him
Whispering to my sister,
"Don't tell anyone about me."
The whisper was witnessed
Only then was his paradise closed.
No more children as his candy.

(The current chaotic times are triggering the
hypervigilance like my childhood.)

STATIC STATE of ANXIETY

I have known constant hypervigilance,
Early in my life,
Turned on to full volume
For five frantic years.
It never consumed me so much
That others would see or know.
Through the constant stress
Of a relationship that should never
Have happened,
Through years of nursing,
I appeared continuously cool.
Through, migraines, spinal leaks and cancer,
I saw with clear eyes,
The depth and breadth of
Current issues and crisises.
I knew the action and which protocol
To use in taming the problem,
But this era of my life.
Are filled with chronic chaos
My life so full I'm flooded,
My orderable world is out of control,
Anxiety attacks are in a static state
Piling up massively,
Problems unaddressed,
In a tsunami of trouble and worry.
The breath and life knocked
Out of my body and
I'm losing strength

To fight for air and,
Starving from lack of nourishment
Buried in the depths
Of distress and stress.
Drowning in the depths.
I pray for hope and help.

(My country is in chaos filled with constant confusion of
facts and controlled answers offered.)

INTRODUCTION TO POEMS FROM MICAH MASON'S FACEBOOK

Doing some of my therapy poetry is like opening Pandora's box, the difference is that I already know the contents when I start to write the poem. It is less scary. I can pick the item up and look at it from all sides, listen to it, and smell it safely now because it is from the past and is less toxic. I can name it and I can make a plan to deal with it unlike in the past. I have since then learned more ways to fit solutions to the issue which makes it easier to understand why it was traumatizing in that past time, but now it is neutralized. It is so much safer to discuss constructively what needs to be done to heal the wounds and better understand the nature of the wound. My counselor can better support and assist me toward healing patterns. It is also now a shared plan of action instead of when I was so much younger. Back then I was hiding the events leaving me in constant pain with a festering wound. While writing the poem I can open Pandora's box and I find HOPE inside. I do this through stream of consciousness poetry. I just let my feelings and/or memories flow freely without judgement concerning my earlier actions. It is like flushing out a physical wound as a nurse. Flushing solutions are frequently saline like our tears which flush out emotional wounds. My poetry is a part of my remedy along with my counselor who is a guide and support person.

PEDOPHILE'S PARADISE

Living on a private street
Loaded with kids,
Boys and girls,
Divided between five houses.
More who come from
Other nearby streets,
For sports and other play
With babies, toddlers, and pre-teens.
There is also a man
Not a stranger with candy,
We were the candy
In a store full of merchandise.
I spent my childhood
In a pedophile's paradise
Until someone caught him
Whispering to my sister,
"Don't tell anyone about me."
The whisper was witnessed
Only then was his paradise closed.
No more children as his candy.

(The current chaotic times are triggering the hypervigilance like my childhood.)

TEMPORARILY CLEAN

The snow freezing traffic
Slowing life's pace
Giving time to look around,
All about the ground,
Trees and sky are white
The brightness of the sun
Shining through sparkling
On every snowflake,
Making the neighborhood
Noticeably cleaner
Under the glistening layer,
Is hidden mud and leaf piles,
Even residual weeds
Below fluffy mounds of pearly white.
Leaving a temporary clean
Abounding all over the ground.

(This was after an unexpected 14 inches of snow fall in
one day.)

TRUST FACTORS

All my current issues
Go back to trust.
Mostly lack of trust:
Trust in people being safe,
Trust in pills being safe,
Trust in food being safe.
Lack of environmental trust,
Leading to stress
And anxious distress.

Adrenal driven hypervigilance
In everything in my present
Loss of life control
Leading to loss of weight
With loss of strength.
I search for self-control
In body and brain,
I don't trust

My judgement it may be
Delusion skewing decisions.
My path to trust
Is in retraining my brain
To recognize truth,

By removing the filtered
Lenses of my world vision
To clearly see the facts.

In hallucinized current times
My blinders need removal
To see the real as real.
The trustable is near
Within my trust zone.

(I am reverting to my childhood lack of trust and need to
travel back to the present and my own current control.
Therapy is the answer when life's setbacks occur.)

FORGIVENESS FOR ME

I am on a path for forgiveness
I find I have forgiven some,
But one was never on the list,
I never forgave myself:
For being a child,
Naïve and sheltered,
Not understanding the world.
I felt stupid, for not knowing;
I felt guilty, for being complicate;
I felt ashamed, for allowing;
I felt used, for believing lies;
I felt self-angered, for not saying NO!
I felt weak, for not being strong;
I felt ugly, for lack of self-esteem;
I felt unwanted, for being a pariah;
I felt contaminated, for being touched;
Beneath my own standards
I was unacceptable by anyone
Confirmed by peers and others
In my mind.

(No one knew, but me. Why would anyone reject me?
Because I closed up and was stand-offish was the more
likely reason stayed at a distance.)

MOURNING MY LIFE

Someone was mourning my life
Before I was dead,
Trying to warn me
My life is in danger.
Now leading me on the paths
Toward safe passages
People around me
Some I know,
Others recently found.
The danger is one
Wobbly step away.
Now a hand is pulling me
Away from the edge,
Back to the healing zone.
There to no need for mourning,
If my course is changed,
With a mindset change.
The safety net grows larger,
With faith and hope
As guard rails,
Are resetting the perimeters
For formational growth,
Toward a golden growth
Of mental homeostasis.

(I finally recognized I was hiding my depression from
my conscious self. To recognize that is a step to getting
help, which I did.)

THE HEALING GOES ON

I didn't recognize,
When I got on the slippery slope
And started moving downward,
Faster and faster,
The incline increased the speed
Accelerating the negative action,
Falling forward
Into a passive position,
Of suicide by non-reaction.
I had to stop me,
Before I got past the point
Of no return or reversal.
Look in the mirror,
What is in the face you see?
This is fractionally what you are
There is more there,
In the depth of your actions
The caring you never engaged,
Giving in to emptiness,
You just generate more emptiness.
Giving for others in need.
Who needs you now?
You need to save your life.
Healing is your duty now,
And for you forever.
You need to be alive and well
To help others in need of care.
(Frustrated because I'm letting myself lose control of my
life.)

RINGING MEMORY

The reminiscence of his
Invasion into my life,
Is with me every day
With the ringing ears,
And limited hearing,
Yet his hearing problems
Were older than mine,
It started as early
As we met.

He was deaf to my messages,
That his behavior was
Unacceptable and over-whelming.
When he pressed too much
To be all of my life
And still never heard NO!

I slowly took 47 aspirin
Over an hour to block
His painful invasion
Of my personal space.

The relationship was as dead,
As the sound of my NO!
Get out of my life!
Stay out of my life!

All these 47 years,
My ever-ringing ears,
Scream out constant noise
Reminding me of wanting out
Of a life filled with him,
Though he's been gone
So many years now.
The scars of my ears
Remind me of his damage.

(My doctor hospitalized me to flush the aspirin out, but
the damage was already done to the nerves in my ears.
He was told to get out of my life and still he continued to
invade by visits and phone calls. He was obsessed with
me and treated me like he owned me. A possessive and
obsessive stalked replaced whatever soul he had.)

INSURRECTION

Insurrection incited by,
The coup-coup president.
Protests rose to riots.
Windows of opportunity
Opened by a failure
Of leadership
To lead safely
And responsibly.
Urges to fight fraud
That never existed.
Deluded and weak,
Urges to fight the
Battle that couldn't be won,
Because there is no war.
Lying was expected
And accepted,
Because of other
Of his own lies,
Needing protection,
And more support
For believers to believe.
To hold delusion,
And its illusion
As if it were true.
Covid is a hoax!
For making America great
As democracy dies,
Eroded by every lie,

While disrespecting
America and its people.
Impeachment's time
Has met the need.
Now complete the Impeachment,
Incomplete in the past,
Stop his future runs
For future elections forever.

(Trump promised to go with the Trumpites which he
didn't do after inciting an insurrection, causing
destruction and four deaths at the time. All this about
fake election fraud and 360,000 COVID deaths he let
happen.)

PATIENCE ZONE

Patience, please!
Pacing is important
To expand horizons
Step by step
Slowly and safely
Because leaping ahead
Sets me back too far;
The space is too scary!
Keep the place secure
When my balance
Is dizzying and unequal
Falls are more common.
My footing is lost.
Without advancement
Achievability is possible
Patience, please!
Let me set my timing
When the period is right
Then I am alright.

(For fear of my health, others try to push me into their safety zone, which may be too hazardous for me right now. Know yourself without delusion and your pacing will match your need. Reality checks with a counselor are strongly advised. Delusions are all too common with physical and mental stress.)

WEIGHING IN ON ISSUES

I lost too much weight
Heavy with tons of stress.
I'm weighing in on
Consequences of more loss.
Weighing choices of food
Heavily planning diets,
To add the bulk I need
To nourish my body,
With balanced fats, carbs
Proteins, vitamins, and minerals.
Healing the loss of weight,
So much of me is gone.
I need to regain, to be me again.
The whole not half.
Weighty problems reduced
To fill up with normalcy,
And better weighing the issues
Of importance to digest,
Or lose them as a toxic diet
Flushing my body of all waste
Lose the weight of stress
Refill with spiritual food
Holistically nourishing.

(I lost way too much weight from stress and food phobia.
Appointments with allergists, nutritionist, and mental
health counselors are helping me weigh out issues to
reduce unnecessary loads of stress and problems. Some
issues just need to be lost from our body, mind, and life.)

PATHETIC PUNK PRESIDENT

Panic! Panic! Panic!
Congress needs to complete
Initiation of the impeachment.
It's so dangerous with delays,
Huge hazardous harm,
Time ticks tediously,
Retaliation needs restraint.
Destroyer of democracy,
Corrupting chaos king.
Pathetic president
Punishing the people,
With disease deaths,
With damage deaths.
Love ME or lay in your grave.
Petty punk of a person.

(After the coup riot, Congress moved for another
impeachment on most corrupt and destructive petty
want-to-be dictator, I had yet another panic attack
worrying that they won't complete it this time either.
And they didn't. I was soothed by a daily dose of L-
Theanine. I also watched happy movies. There was
breathing exercises that can help.)

THE BRIDGE OF OBSTRUCTION

Teetering on the edge of the end,
I hung on the overpass bridge,
The car frame balanced on the rail
As a highway patrolman
Came to check my status
As we waited for help to arrive.
I was floating above my city.
Falsely feeling safe,
I was facing my potential death,
But feeling no fear,
Filling with frustration
I needed to get to work
My clients needed my help.
Rocking on a bridge
Was not on my schedule.
Number one tow truck . . .
The boom was too short.
Number two tow truck . . .
The boom still too short.
Number three tow truck . . .
The semi-boom was successful.
I was off the bridge rail
Safely on terra firma.
The only donut I had had
That cold morning
Was a donut spin on ice.

(I used my "stuck" time to call my patients to assure them that I would get there as soon as I could due to an accident. I was more concerned about messing up my schedule. I hadn't thought about how high up I was and if the car went over the rail I would be seriously hurt or die. My patients always came first.)

CAR POOL FOG

Traveling in a blanket of dense fog,
Visibility was less than the hood.
Seeing none of my neighborhood
Night had us trapped in a clog.
We three edged to the rail road.
No safety gate or light,
Not a star so bright,
Broke through that night.
To warn of the danger
That moved on the track.
The dense fog smothered the scene
Of what was a fast train,
The danger we would greet
Invisible, stealthy, and silent.
It moved with great force,
Only I sensed death present.
Flying on that track
I pulled back and stopped.
Though the others were unhappy,
Protesting I budged not an inch,
Stubbornly staying against their anger.
Minutes as a hostage of the unseen,
The monster was real and present.
I felt the eminent death and destruction.
Protests continued from the tired riders,
After hours of work,
Their highest priority was sleep,
Knowing the danger blocking us

The wait was on-going,
Then a light in the dark night
Showed what I already knew,
All along by a car on
The other side of the track,
A train had been there,
Speeding with stealth and silence.
Crossing the track would have been
Certain, sudden death.

(My sixth sense knew the train was flying through the
intersection though those gals never had a clue until the
other car's lights showed the real present danger. I might
have felt some ground tremble in the steering wheel, but
I trusted my gut feeling and saved all their lives. They
had extra long trains along there after midnight.)

COUP BY CULT

So, so very sad,
The simpering baby man,
Needed the presidency repeated,
To keep from paying
Millions of dollars of loans.
He dared not lose
With so much at stalk,
To get a big break,
He called it a fake.
He could not lose,
So, he planned a coup,
To steal the election,
Was a must . . .
It was only just,
Justice for him but,
Not for the country.
Destroying its safety by,
Building a wall of lies.
The only wall he completed.
Controlling crowds of cultists,
With subliminal mafia speak
He coaxed them to treason
Taking no reasonable
Responsibility to incite, and
Encourage their bad
And dangerous behavior.
Praising and protecting people,
Who planned and practiced

Many months of mayhem,
To crush the Capitol,
And demolish democracy.
All for his failed businesses,
Practiced by not paying
Bills and loans.
Steal an election
By lying about fraud,
While disrupting mail ballots,
Shutting voter sites,
Suing about frauds
That never happened.
Deluding public vision
By constant twitter feed,
The faithful cultist
Followed his instructions,
To aid his traitors' coup.
All this to keep from
Paying bills and loans due.
Weren't his grifts and lies
Bringing enough money making,
Adequate to be solvent,
That's some "art of the deal".

(Trump's thinking reminds me of my son's ADHD and
more. Impulsive actions without consideration of
consequences. Records show he was not a good
businessman.)

FOOD FEAR

It is hard to have an appetite.
Just to swallow a bite
Your throat grows so tight.
The texture too tough,
Too sandy rough,
To set off a cough,
And then the choke
On what you partook.

Food is the enemy you cook.
The smell, the taste,
To inviting to waste,
While still warm to haste
Crispy and flaky bread,
Crusty, then chewy instead.

Buttery sweet melted spread
Or savory tomato and cheese
Perfect pizza to please,
To down like a swarm of bees
Now unsafe torture.

No more loving nurture,
Gone is the usual nature
Of great smells to craving,
The taste others are raving,
Too scary for braving.
When food is a punishment
And not a fine refreshment.

(I'm still fighting food phobia that interfere with my
eating habits. I was always a foodie.)

SAFE CHOICE?

Still no self-trust,
To choose the safe item,
To

choose the safe people,
To choose the safe place,
To choose the safe food,
To choose the safe word.
Am I safe to choose safe?
Am I capable,
To make the choice?

(I still don't feel safe to eat alone. Will I have a reaction
or choke?)

WISHING

Tears for the missing
And me just wishing,
For the food's flavor,
And tastes I savor,
But my throat won't accept.
I wish I could except,
Throat scares or soreness,
Because swallowing business
Of food swallowing,
And my stomach hallowing
I gotten so skinny.
I'm in sizes mini,
While I really want to savor
All of great food's flavor.
But with slim choices,
No matter the voices.
Food lost most of its charm,
Due to the layer of harm.
I search therapy to heal,
To enjoy a great meal.

(More doctors, more tests, but I'm finding more answers
to get to better health and putting meat on my bones.)

PARASITIC

Once you latched on to me
You refused to leave.
You pushed away my friends.
You made them uncomfortable.
They didn't want to stay.
When that didn't work,
You isolated and insulated me.
From any others contacts.
You brainwashed to empty,
So, there was nothing, but you.
You filled my space and time
Trying to fill your emptiness.
You glued and glued
Yourself into and around,
My life with your toxins.
Your parasitic poisons,
To paralyze my life and
To more easily attach,
And break me down
To absorb all of me,
To fill all your emptiness.
Let me be free, free of you
I don't need a parasitic growth
To be whole
I am whole by myself.
(Travis grafted himself on to me and my life because he
felt so empty. He was smothering me with his presence
everywhere in my life. He took over my life every
weekend. It was hard to see friends or family.)

REFUSED TO RECEIVE

While you refused to receive,
You never understood
Why you could not see me,
During "that spring",
I did not want to be with you,
Not ever, ever again
I took all the aspirins,
So, you would not see me,
Not ever, ever again.
You would not leave,
Never, never when I asked.
I told you so often to get out,
But you rejected the messages.
Since you would not leave,
It seemed up to me to leave.
So, I took all the aspirins,
Again, and again to empty
The contents of the bottle.
You would not leave,
So, I chose to leave myself.

(I tried so many times to get him to go out of my life. He
refused to understand my message of rejection. Which
made him just dig in deeper to get more attached to my
life and controlling my choices.)

BOOGERS BE GONE

Some people are like boogers,
They fill up spaces
So, you can't breathe
So, with tissue in hand
That you blow to remove
You dive in to get it
Still without success.
That obstruction is there,
But it won't budge,
So, you dig a little more
Until you can breathe.
Then you've pulled that
Bad booger out,
And you'll be free
To breathe again,
But now you can't
Get that clinging glob
Off your finger.
It just doesn't want
To leave.
Take a hint,
Booger be gone.

(Some people get into your life and suck up all the air
and fill all the space. You try and try to politely remove
them, but they refuse to leave. Even when you remove
them physically, they cling to parts of your life.)

DRAGON-EYE MOON

During the dragon-eye moon,
When the cloud forms a dragon,
Things can be strange,
Light can change.
There's a presence
In residence,
It's not just illusion
Or even delusion,
On those nights
With limited lights,
The dragon sees his realm
His power will overwhelm.
He rules the sky,
Lord-like from high.
The dragon has always been
Even when not seen,
Like the rare blue moon
Rarer is the dragon-eye moon.

(Some of natures pictures are rare like aurora borealis
seen in Ohio or Pennsylvania, or ball lightning. Other
pictures of nature need a creative mind like seeing
dragons in the night sky in cloud formation with an extra
bright moon. Keep your mind active and creative, it will
keep you young.)

TOO MUCH ICK

The constant state
Of low level frantic,
Has slide out of frame
And the fear of panic
Has gone out of trend.
Since the master manic
Doesn't lead the land.
Reduced events of havoc
Are few and rare.
Mostly residual cultic,
Mindsets that persist
A fewer surface cyclic
As fact not relic
The recent events
Real and historic,
Changing a country
In a gross epic,
From lying leaders,
Inciting hysterics.

(For four years the patients have been taking over the
asylum and its been running on delusions and manic
meanness and mindsets of exclusion and tribalism. "Join
us", or we'll destroy you, "hate-think". The negativity is
wearing as it uses up positivity.)

ON THE MENU

Migraines are a daily special,
Weather permitting.
Usually starting in one quarter-sized
Spot on the top of my head,
Generally, the left temple.

Slowly expanding to fill the hemisphere
With unquestionable pain.
Early-bird special may include:
Neck pain as appetizer starters,
Or headaches that extend,
To full meals of neck pain.

There are also the unappetizing:
Starters of nausea,
That fill in the spaces,
Unsatiated by head pain.
Surprise specials of pre-headache:
Auras of bi-ocular,
Light and color shows,
Filling the visual field.

Occasional option changes include:
Veiling a partial view,
Left-sided only auras,
For a similar obstruction.
A rare offering years apart:
Is the total blindness,

Suddenly occluding vision,
For fifteen to sixty minutes,
Years ago, a week-long limit:
Presented left-sided weakness,
Without numbness,
Or most of a day.
During that same time:
Lock-jaw tight muscles,
Lack of left tongue control,
Made speech difficult.
These side-order options vary:
Come without choices,
Never warned on a menu,
Unexpected plate filers.
To confuse the migraine issue:
Some of the side dishes,
Come alone without a headache.

(One famous headache specialist suggested some of the symptoms were likely basilar in nature. Others offered trigeminal nerve problems as the root cause of some specific symptoms.)

THE SOLUTION MENU

Early choice of Dristan,
Usually worked well.
Aspirins were available,
But much less effective.
Depend on the weather change,
Cold cloth or warm.
Prescription medications,
Offered limited aid.
Botox injections numbed,
A halo ring with pain above.
Inderal was offered but,
My blood pressure was too low.
Effexor with other meds,
Lessened pain sometimes.
Zanaflex help tone down,
Neck and jaw-tightness.
Caffeine helped more consistent,
But increased jumpiness.
An herbal home-made blend,
Helped with early use.

(Weather induced migraine headaches are tricky to
treat. There are no one-pill-solution fits all headaches
situation. Adding to this issue climate change also has
spawn a wider type and cause of my headaches. Each
headache is more trial and error to achieve treatment
success.)

PASSIVE SUICIDE

Passive suicide,
Is still suicide.
The end goal is the same
Death of the body
Or end of life.

It only depends on
Which is most offensive,
The body
Or the life?
Which do you
Wish to be rid of,
Body you were born with
Or body you let happen?

Life choices OR
Life satisfaction?
Life ends with the body's end.
Body's end with life's end.
How do you end it?
Neglect of care,
Over eat? Under eat?

Alcohol, drugs, smoking
Over-indulgence
Can be neglect
Through nutrition-less
And nurture-less life.

Healthful care is missing
Neglectful maintenance
Is a path to death
Cell by cell,
Or organ by organ,
It leads to death
Time is the greatest factor
Long or short interval
Passive suicide is a
Slippery slope that
Moves past the point
Of no return
Passively out of control
Recognition brings back control
Put on the brakes,
Or change the course,
Control is still there.
Make a choice,
Choosing is control.
Choosing is action.
If you are actively involved,
You are in charge
There is NO passive suicide.

(Passive suicide is a relinquishing of control. Never give
up control. Get a therapist to help make choices.)

FLY FROM STRESS

Worry for my son's health.
Worry for other's lack of wealth.
Friends without jobs,
Others who will lose jobs.
Best friend leaving the state.
Without her, what is my fate?
Finding next people of support.
Worse with family of no support.
Emptiness is leaving a void,
Prematurely trying avoid.
Shutting down to super freeze,
Wishing numbness was a breeze.
It's painful in my chest
Finding coping symptoms at best.
Smothered in layers of stress.
My body is in distress.
I wish I could be a butterfly,
Cocooning until I can fly,
To a better place
In a safe space.

(I'm having an increase in moderate and high levels of
stress. Swallowing problems are increasing with the
stress so that increases stress. My son's health is in
jeopardy and a dear friend is moving out of state. She has
been my important support system member along with
my son.)

SHARED STRESS

MY son is STRESSED!
By his allergy test
Afraid without his Epi-pen.
With needing to know he's open,
Traffic to the doctor
Is a terrific horror,
So, he'll persevere the hell
That knowing will tell.
Allergen unknown factor
Are a scarier mental factor.
His stress becomes my stress,
And my stress is his stress.
Feeding the flames of fears
I let loose a flood of tears.
I wish it cleanses my body
Knowing he's safe in his body.
With answers soon known
And a short list of unknown.

(I'm stressed about my son's longer list of allergies
presently. Unusual combo's in many foods, so all labels
need to be carefully read. Fragrances in personal and
household cleaning supplies, and more are suspect until
proven safe.)

THE ESCAPE DOOR

Years ago, I tried to escape
Through a door where no one
Passes through twice.
This is a once passed through
There is no return door.
But I was pulled back,
Before the door was locked.
I am a suicide survivor.
Though I don't have,
Visible scars,
I have mental and physical scars.
Hearing damage from
An overdose of aspirins,
And depression from feeling
Trapped in a life that,
Wasn't my plan,
In a relationship that won't end.
My alternative plan was
The escape door.
Thankfully, it was locked,
So, I couldn't
Get through,
And I found alternative plans.
My lesson learned was . . .
There are always other choices.

(My boyfriend was too controlling and wasn't willing to
receive my messages to get out of my life. So, I poorly
decided to go to a place he won't be able to go. As I
recovered, I realized that he was possessive and would
later be known as a stalker type.)

SOUR MILK

Sour milk saved my life
A sore stomach
Crying for relief,
Filled with 47 aspirins.
It burned like a bonfire.
My gripping and complaining,
Alerted a classmate's attention.
I confessed the pain
Was from too many aspirins
My doctor was called,
My mother was called.
Too late for a stomach pump.
I was drown with IV's.
My body was flushed.
So, I could live.
Saved by a carton
Of sour milk,
And a dear classmate.

(I would have just let it go on until it was too late if my
stomach was calmed by that milk. I'd have gone to bed,
to sleep through to the grave.)

STANDING TALL

Standing straight and tall,
I look upward to the sky
My chin firmly set.
I am strongly aware,
Proud of my bravery.
Life's hazards didn't
Break me then,
I am stronger within.
Every life crisis
Fertilized my resolve.
My core foundation is fortified,
More ready for the next event,
Better and better each time.
Physically and emotionally bruised,
But never broken.

(My visualization of myself strong and brave for now
and the future. I am stronger after every life event.)

MID-APRIL SNOW

Before the curtains
Are drawn open,
I know it snowed.
I heard the salt trucks,
Blades scraping the road.
It's April 21, 2021!
Open curtains reveal
Two inches of snow
On the grass,
That was green
Yesterday, just yesterday!
Fluffs of white
Cover every branch
Pink apple blossoms
Peek through white.
The planet has lost
All normalcy.
A strange new earth
Gone the earth
Of my youth.

(Climate change damage expands each year.)

CLIMATE CHANGE IS REAL!

There is climate change
It hurts me with
Weather change migraines
Before, only spring and fall,
But now every season
Under the sun.
Migraine pain year-round,
Any day or month,
Volatile weather.
No more a respite,
During summer and winter.
I not only see the
Climate changing,
I feel it every day.
So, deny away!
It's here to stay.
Wake up to reality.

(My migraines remind me climate change is real.)

MORAL LEPER

As a child,
I felt like
A moral leper.
Unclean,
Sullied,
Unacceptable,
Because,
He touched me.
I was then,
A contaminate
In the world.
A personal plague
On society,
Untouchable,
Unclean.

(When children are molested repeatedly, they feel like
they are the bad one, but he was the contaminating
moral leper.)

WHAT I SEE

The mirror is there,
But I want dare
To look at me.
Fearing what I see,
Old and worn
Not a face adorn
Baring the strife
Of a life,
Events now born
In a crown of thorn.
Head bent low
My body my foe.
If there is beauty
It is brain bounty,
A life of other's care
And being fair.

(I still have trouble looking at myself in the mirror, due
to poor self-esteem. Teasing by peers and the past abuse
still hides in the shadows of my mind.)

HOLLOW VESSEL

Hollow, empty people
With no self-esteem
Frequently put on air
Of supreme arrogance
And self-importance.
They need praise
To fill their empty
Vacuumous spaces.
They seek center stage
And huge crowds,
But they are
Never filled
So, they demand
More constantly,
But still they
Can never
Feel fulfilled,
Or self-satisfaction.
They are the wounded
Perma-victims
Stuck inside their
Empty vessel of self-doubt.

(Some people are so greedy for attention and adoration,
because they are empty vessels of hopeless humanity.
They don't have enough self-esteem to feed their own
need for self-fulfillment.)

VAX TO RELAX

I got my vax,
Now I can relax,
One by one, I do
Till I have two.
How about you?
Still need my mask,
To keep up the task
Of not sharing covid
As I did
In the past year
To protect those dear
For my family
And your family.
Everyone should
And they could,
So, why don't they
Instead of nay-say.

(There were too many who didn't believe in or trust the vaccines, so they didn't go get one. Many more got sick or died due to that mindset.)

ORIANA

Better than Mona Lisa's smile.
The sun hides in shame,
Her smile makes the day shine,
And it makes my heart shine.
No need for tears or rain
There is joy and laughter
In that special smile.
Hope for tomorrow reigns
Healing is possible in the now.
Step by step, smile by smile.
The light of her smile
Shows the pathway to change.

(Oriana is the golden dawn of my new beginning
reincarnated to a new start of a new me even better.)

ABSENT HERO

He could have been
The hero I needed.
Not to have to be
The permanent one,
But to be the one
Who split the other,
Away and out of
Any part of my life,
But he was disinterested,
In me or my plight.
I invited him to come
And be my changer,
But he ignored my plea,
Not understanding,
The chance to heal
My bruised and wounded
Emotions and life,
By incising a parasite
That was infesting
And affecting my life,
In a most negative way.
Why did you ignore my call
For help?
Then later be so mad,
Because you weren't
Invited to the event,
That could have changed
Both of our lives?

Even if we never
Stayed permanently
In the same circle.
Don't be vexed at me,
When you ignored
A chance to be my hero,
While you missed
The fun the others
Had and bragged about.
You had a chance
At great things
You dismissed,
By not coming
When you were invited.
Did you really forget
When I welcomed you?
Were you so preoccupied,
Or just refused to be
In my presence
That day with the others?
You could have been
My hero and save me,
From present and future danger.

(I invited a number of people from work to a picnic, but
the only one who didn't come was the one I wanted
most. And years later he was the only one angry with
me. The only one who ignored my welcoming invitation.
I actually invited him a day before I gave others their
invitations.)

HIS SMELL

Nasty assault to the nose
Sickly sour
With unnatural
Over-whelming sweetness.
Poorly washed
Never smelling clean.
Repulsive, repugnant
It clung to me
Like he did.
It fills my memory
In a negative way.
Why can't I wash
Him away?
The strained times,
Like I strain,
To remove,
That sickly sour sweet smell.

(His mother couldn't properly clean his clothes because
his father didn't fix the hot water heater. His father
worked maintenance at his company and fixed
everybody's water heater and furance around the
county, but didn't put his own house in order.)

THE WRITER'S AWARD

The prize!
The prize!
I'm hoping for a prize.
To show myself,
And many others,
My worth,
My talents,
Are very visible.
Not quietly invisible,
Not small and divisible,
It is a whole
Of all of me.
I am a crafter
Of words and fiber
With my active brain.

(I have applied for a writer's award for my poetry book. I pray I will be recognized for one of the awards.)

VERONICA'S HOME

I stand in the cold rain
Shivering part . . .
From the drizzling cold,
And from the loss,
Emptiness from the
Hole which Veronica
Used to fill.
Here on the dreary day,
She goes to her
Final home
The cemetery plot,
Her soul free-floating
Without the body,
That bound her
To the surface of the earth.
Now she is wherever,
And everywhere
She wishes.

(This is a memory of my feeling at her funeral at the
grave side.)

THE RAIN OF LIES

Trump's magical kingdom of lies,
Lies about COVID,
Even after he was
On death's doorstep
From respiratory failure,
Lied about people,
Stealing the election.
When he was trying
To steal the election,
By messing with the mail service.
Encouraging voter suppression.
Lying about the votes,
When it was about
Him not wanting to
Pay off loans.
Lies about all his success,
As the best-ever president.
Lies about all his work,
As he sat on his as
Eating Kentucky fried, and

Absorbing bad news from
Sources of questionable.
Popping amphetamines
And ragging on others,
For what he was doing.
And still he whined
Out piles of lies,

At a new round of rallies.
As long as he lives
The lies spew forth,
From his mouth,
His kingdom is
Sustained by the believer's
Of his lies.
As malevolent as
A lightning storm,
His lies rain on America.

(The bigger the lies and the more they are repeated it becomes imprinted in your brain. It's a form of public brain-washing. Hitler did it constantly.)

MY TWIN, MY HERO

I owe my life
To my twin,
She saw my need
When I did not care,
But she cared.
She got the doctor
To save my life
To keep me alive.
She kept my secret
To keep me in school
My twin withheld
The truth so,
Teachers won't know.
She kept the night vigil
Assuring my safety.
Giving up her sleep,
To keep me from,
The long sleep of death.

(She saw I was taking pills too frequently and questioned
my purpose.)

HIS WINNER'S TROPHY

It was a symbol of his control and power,
To keep me from leaving
When I finally got other cars.
He took mine and left
The ones I couldn't
Or wouldn't drive.
I only got a car work on days.
The message was,
I was expected to work,
And bring in a paycheck,
Which he usually controlled,
By leaving me the bills to pay.
It was always about
Power and control.

(It took me fifteen years to realize the broken
transmission on my car was his control of my potential
leaving him again. Ultimately, I divorced him and moved
an hour drive away from him. I did it without a car for 18
months. I finally own my own life and control to leave or
stay.)

ENERGY STEALING CLIMATE

If you have:
Migraines,
Muscle aches,
Or arthritis,
Climate change instability
Is a hellish life,
With pain levels that
Are just as instable
As the weather.
Constant temperature change
Low pressure, high pressure
Humid or arid.
Which will it be?
How long will it last?
Long enough for my body
To acclimate?
Chances are NO!
It makes for misery
In all aspects of life.
Always in a state of
Depression and blues.
Pulling the last
Bits of vitality
Out of my life.

(I can't downplay the reality of climate change it messes
with my life on a daily basis. Weather reports can be
scarier than a horror movie, especially when listening to
a week-long predication.)

WHATEVER IT TAKES

Heating pads,
And cold clothes,
Strategically placed
To make the head pain reduce
To a tolerable level,
So, life as I want it to be
Can proceed.
So, the invalid state
Is staved off;
For minutes,
Or hours,
So, life can go on
With normalcy,
As such can be achieved,
During the trauma,
Drama of migraines,
Otherwise, energy is zapped
To emptiness,
And I'd be bed-bound
Most of my life.
An invalid invalid,

A worthless, space stealing nothingness.
(I hate feeling like a worthless space filler.)

NO SEWING MACHINE NOW

Migraines and sewing machines
Don't work together,
So, I hand-sew to distract.
From all the head pain
Keeping my brain busy
I make stacks of stuff
Clothes, quilts, and more
Being productive
Keeps me less depressive
Making time go by.

(I really need to feel useful at all cost.)

A DOOR TO CONTROL

A door ajar,
And he came in
Refusing to leave,
He took my life controlling:
My time,
My space,
My life.
Locking the door
To all others;

Isolating,
Insulating,
My life was filled
With his presence;
His opinions,
His wishes,
His desires,
Until he crushed
As much of me
As he could control

Without respect;
For my opinion,
For my desires,
For my wishes.
He made it uncomfortable

To be in my circle;
Isolation in space,
Isolation in relationship,
Isolation from nurture,
Breaking me,
Controlling me.

(My greater need for independence grew stronger for the sake of my survival, so I filed for divorce finally, but he didn't give up easily, never signing the divorce papers.)

HATE OF LIFE

Hate of being alive.
Resenting his life,
Coming from a relation
That never should
Have happened.
We share a hate of life.
Never wishing to be born
Into the life,
Fate gave us.
Considering chosen exits,
Or changes.
Trying to change lie's course.
To be a tolerable,
Acceptable of life's experience.
Controlling as much
Possible as one can.
When control is not possible,
Learning coping methods,
Searching new pathways.
Life is a journey
With multiple paths,
And destinations.
Life doesn't need to
Stay the same.

(When life isn't working, be unafraid to make change.
Bravery moves change forward.)

AMERICA SINKS

The Titanic was too big to sink,
And yet –
It did sink completely.
America believes
It is too big,
And too powerful
To sink into oblivion,
But a virus,
And uncaring leaders,
Will be our iceberg.
Corrosive, corruption
Will sink us below
The safe water-line.
While we ignore
The collision with democracy.
We drown in lies,
And false beliefs.
Watching America die,
We knew it can die, too.

(If we keep believing the lies and not vetting out the
facts we can go down like the Titanic.)

TROPHY OF CONTROL

A sign of my hubby's disrespect.
Went home to mom after work.
Weeks later Mr. Passive-aggressive,
Ripped up the transmission
Of the car, I spent three years
Summer work to save.
The broken car was kept
At the first and then,
The second house.
Fifteen years of a rusting
Unfixed car waiting for repair.
The township zoning rules,
Finally forced its removal.
So why was it unfixed?
Because it was his trophy of
Control to keep me from
Leaving him.

(When I realized the symbol as a trophy of controlling
my ability to be mobile and leave independently it added
to my desire to get divorced. This was inappropriate
control over another person.)

THE PRICE OF LIFE

Used up and tired,
Is where I live,
And have lived
Many years with my son.
We share the life stressors.
Life has been . . .
Physically and emotionally
Hard and very wearing.
I feel and my son feels,
Eroded to the core.
Energy emptying endlessly,
We are vacant vessels
In great need of filling;
With love, care,
Food, refueling sleep.
General health, and balance.
Make us holistically whole.
So, we can find peace and calm;
Satisfaction and acceptance;
Awareness of our worth.
And a worth of life.

(Years of over-whelming stress to body and mind, then
COVID was the coup de grace.)

NO COMPUTER BRAIN

I would never ever
Want my brain
Connected to a computer
No streaming thoughts
Pouring into my brain
Full of other's thoughts
NO propaganda,
NO brainwashing,
NO misinformation,
NO computer viruses,
NO internet,
NO bigotry and exclusion.
I want to control my own brain
WITH creativity,
WITH new thoughts,
WITH artistry,
WITH variety,
WITH positivity,
WITH relationships.
A computer doesn't have a
Human style-brain function
It's a cell phone implant.

(I wrote this after watching an episode of "Outer Limits".

NO SOCIAL RELATIONSHIP

Dad had no time for me.
His time was devoted to
Happy hobbies,
To heal the wounds
Of his hated job.
His great share was vacations,
Adventures in wild America
And it's beauty on hikes.
But there was no relationship.

Mom feed me clothed me,
And cared for my health.
She taught me how to:
Sew, knit, cook, and
Clean my living space;
She helped with homework,
She introduced me to a faith walk.
But there was no relationship.

My sisters were athletic.
Caring more about appearance:
Make-up, hair-styles, and clothes.
They had more friends,
Both girls and boys.
There was an unacknowledged
Competition, always on going.
But there was no relationship.

We existed in the same space,
But rarely interacted,
More like playtime
For toddlers with parallel-play,
Not crossing invisible lines
To help build cabins or castles.
Just sharing a space.
Interacting or acting
Only on specific requests.

(It was like living in a boarding house or hotel. Everyone had their understood space, roles, and jobs. There was no need to interact, as long as you did your part, by the rules or request. There was no necessary social interaction except for respect of others private space. I was physically nurtured, but I didn't feel emotionally nurtured. I believe my sisters did.)

MY REPEATING HISTORY

I don't care how I look.
If I improve.
Most don't notice,
With wallflower invisibility.
Those who do notice
Are critical of my flaws,
Perceived by them,
And feared by me.
So, I give up
Without self-care,
And survival in mind.
Frumpy clothes to put off others,
Don't brush my teeth, so,
Put off by bad breath and cavities
No make-up.
Hair brushed without style,
I'm in agreement with them.
They don't like me, and
I don't like me.
Negativity in agreement,
I crawl back into the wallpaper,
Where the flowers accept me,
And I feel safe,
From critical reviews.
Invisible, devoid of attention,
Hurt only by neglect,
And absent of positivity.
As flat as the wall,

Where I cling,
Empty of the food of friendship,
But not wounded by foes,
Quietly, I fill the room
With a beauty from
The flowers surrounding me
That grow fruits of my art.
The multiple crafts
Anonymously shared.
There from afar I hear
Their praise,
Without the critical
Review of my presence.
I stay on the wall
Of passive survival,
Invisible from the danger.

(It's hard to never fit in with family and peers. Only the most perceptive were aware of my worth and gravitated to me. They were safe to let into my world. Reaching out to others first made me as desirable as peeling wallpaper.)

MY HOARDER'S HOUSE

My house looks like a warehouse,
Of craft supplies
And resource books,
All of many genres.
It is a hoarder's paradise,
Or maybe a prison.
Doers need supplies
When the need hits,
To produce a craft,
For mine or others,
Need or desire.
Supplies build and pile:
By sales,
By rummage,
By gifting,
By other's ridding.
With my hoard,
I'm ready to go,
For any craft,
Or project,
Convenient for a job, but
Inconvenient for living.

(My hoard collected for my retirement to fill my time
with busy-ness,)

LACK IN ABUNDANCE

We have climate volatility,
With crop vulnerability,
A need for multi-versatility,
Instead, a push for GMO seeds,
That grow plants
With sterile seeds.

Droughts, floods, and fires
Threaten crops of great harvest.
While many push for
Increased people fertility,
Babies born to futility,
And growing poverty.

Pushing bans on contraceptives,
And bans on abortion.
Government cuts in welfare,
To those in greatest need,
While the rich donor's bribes
Buy laws that cut taxes
For corporations and
Two percenters on top.

The top gains more,
With multiplicity,
Full of duplicity,
And complicity,
As the bottom twenty percent

Fall deeper in squalor,
With few needs met.
Too weakened and deprived,
To pull themselves up
They get pushed down further.
As the top gets higher
And unreachable,
The bottom drowning deeper
With that growing population.

(The chances of survival at the bottom grows less likely
as those that have it all hide their hoard unshared.)

THE CAT LADY'S RATIO

The cat lady's ratio determines
How long she will live.
The more she has,
The more years
Of insurance exists
To keep on living.

It's the reason
To live
It's the need
To exist.
She must live on,
As long as,
There are cats
In need of her
Presence to survive.
The more cats
The longer she'll try
To live for their care,
And care for herself,
To care for them.
It's the purpose
To life,
When she has
No desire,
To life for herself,
Or by herself.
It's a passive suicide
Prevention pact.

(My thoughts on why some people have so many pets.
Likely because they need a reason to live.)

THE VIEW BEFORE YOU

Focusing on the view before you,
Don't get lost in opinions
When reality is in front of you.
Opinion moves in emotions
Flowing in the ways of floods,
Covering the situations,
And muddying events
Clouding the truth of facts.
Judgements are too hastily made,
And place on pedestals,
Or buried far too soon.
When brought to light,
The vision is very different,
More careful observation,
May bring a better synopsis
Of with quality decisions.
Stand back, look more,
Judge less quickly.

(This fits almost any decision made on small or large
events or issues.)

DEVOID SOULS

There are those devoid of soul,
With no attachment to humanity.
Removed of all compassion
Or empathy for others.
The neglect or abuse
Those people in the sphere
Associated only by proximity,
Never by human connection,
They may go through motions
That appear to be caring,
But they are never bound
To anyone but themselves.
It's more about visuals
That makes them appear normal,
To fit better into society.
Ultimately, it's about status
And acceptance in community.
It's more about social climbing
Reptilian by nature's standard.

(There are some people who live in community, but
never are part of it because the only work for their own
needs and wants.
This is very reptilian in nature.)

SAGED INSIGHT

Looking at your life,
With grace,
While gratefully
Acknowledging the good.
Counting blessings,
Even the ones that
Seemed like curses,
Grow into gifts:
Of tolerance,
Through patience,
To see the lessons learned.
When looking back
Filled with wisdom,
And surprising joy,
Hydrating the dry
Old parts of life
Gone past,
But not fully dead.
As this knowledge touches
Heart and mind
More aware of how
To face events,
In future times,
With a sage's insights
To handle that future
Better than the past.

(While watching the movie "The Shack", I forgave my
opinions of my past and felt more tolerant of how I
navigated those times gone by and counted blessings of
lessons learned.)

USED UP

A used-up person
Worn out by life,
Birth defects,
Physical illness,
Mental illness
Life-threatening events,
People using my kindness,
People using my caring,
People using my talents,
Little given back in kind
Leaving me an empty vessel.
A vessel cracked
Leaking too much,
Empty of hope and peace.
I pray for healing and balance
For change in my life.

(I sometimes feel sad from an emptiness in certain part
of my being and my life. Pray fills me.)

EPILOGUE:

I encourage all readers of this book to exam their life for Adverse Childhood Experiences (ACE's). You may not have been molested or raped, but other experiences can affect your well-being. Chronic emotional, physical, or financial neglect, verbal abuse from volume and word choices from those in your environment can add up to ACE's. Parents or guardians who had their own ACE's can be stressful for their children if they have not counselled to resolve their issues. The first step is recognizing these issues have affected your life and attitudes and that you need to get help. Long-term stresses, mild or severe, can cause amygdala and chronic stress to the adrenals which throws the body into imbalance of many organ systems. This can also lead to a long list of autoimmune diseases such as fibromyalgia, chronic fatigue, arthritis, diabetes and more health issues. Don't let depression, broken spirit, or an imbalanced body wear you down so far that you don't seek help. Even if you have to use your last strength move toward help do it, fight to take your life back. You need to keep working on healing solutions otherwise the abuse continues. Don't let the abusers of this world win.

For more detailed information check out my reading and hymn resource lists and look for my next book "Slow Seduction: A Pedophile's Protocol" for the full story and my whole healing journey.

HYMN RESOURCE LIST:

Even though I wrote poetry to express my feelings. I still clung to or found comfort in my hymns from my church. I frequently found myself humming hymns absent of the awareness that I was in fact humming. I eventually learned that when I repeatedly hummed a particular hymn that I needed to pay closer attention to the songs message. When I repeatedly hummed or sang, "His Yoke Is Easy" from Handel's "Messiah", I usually was overburdened and needed help working through an issue.

I invite you to consider reading, singing, or humming hymns. Especially for those who are not poets or journal writers, they can bring comfort or insight. Fortunately, hymnals have topical indexes, so it is much easier to find a hymn that suits your current need.

People who are molested are not sinners, but sometimes we can go through stages where we feel like a sinner. Or we may have hurt others physically or emotionally when we are in pain. Sometimes it helps to forgive yourself even though you didn't do the misdeed, but you lashed out at another from your inner anger. Hymns can become prayers to open up to healing and feeling worthy of receiving God's or human's help for our healing. I didn't accept God's healing for many years. I thought I knew better than God, but He kept giving me hymns to heal, support, and comfort me until I accepted His healing touch. Sometimes our greatest sin is believing we're not worthy of healing. By making this choice we put ourselves above God. Here are some hymns that helped me by category. I also listed the resources of these hymns, and I coded the specific source with (AG), (WC), and (UMH).

(AG) - Kenneth W. Osbeck. 1990. "Amazing Grace - 366 Inspiring Hymn Stories for Daily Devotions". Grand Rapids, MI: Kregel Publications.

(WC) - _____. 1990. "The Worshiping Church - A Hymnal". Carol Stream, IL: Hope Publishing Company.

(UMH) - _____. 1989. "The United Methodist Hymnal". Nashville, TN: The Methodist Publishing House.

ACCEPTANCE

"And Can It Be That I Should Gain" (UMH)
"His Eye Is On The Sparrow" (AG)
"It's Me, It's Me, O Lord" (UMH)
"No One Understands Like Jesus" (AG)
"Search Me, O God" (WC)
"What Wonderous Love Is This" (WC)
"Why Should He Love Me So?" (AG)

AFFLICTION

"Leave It There" (UMH)
"Precious Lord Take My Hand" (AG)
"Softly And Tenderly, Jesus Is Calling" (WC)
"Standing On The Promises" (AG)

"There Is A Balm In Gilead" (UMH)
"What A Friend We Have In Jesus" (AG)

ASSURANCE

"All My Hope So Firmly Grounded" (UMH)
"Ask Ye What Great Thing I Know" (AG)
"Blessed Assurance" (AG)
"Faith Of Our Fathers" (AG)
"Glorious Things Of Thee Are Spoken" (AG)
"He's Got The Whole World" (WC)
"Immortal, Invisible" (AG)
"It Came Upon The Midnight Clear" (AG)
"O Love That Wilt Not Let Me Go" (UMH)
"This Is My Father's World" (AG)
"Through It All" (UMH)
"What Wonderous Love Is This" (AG)

BLESSINGS

"All Things Bright And Beautiful" (UMH)
"Count Your Blessings" (AG)
"There Shall Be Showers Of Blessings" (AG)

COMFORT

"Are You Weary, Heavy Laden ?" (WC)
"Come, Ye Disconsolate" (AG)
"Come Ye Sinners, Poor And Needy" (WC)
"The Comforter Has Come" (AG)

"Every time I Feel The Spirit" (WC)
"God We'll Take Care Of You" (AG)
"It Is Well With My Soul" (AG)
"Jesus Is All The World To Me" (AG)
"Jesus, Lover Of My Soul" (UMH)
"Kum Ba Yah" (UMH)
"Leaning On The Everlasting Arms" (AG)
"Nearer, My God To Thee" (UMH)
"Nobody Knows The Trouble I See" (UMH)
"Stand By Me" (UMH)
"When All Thy Mercies, O My God" (AG)

COMMITMENT

"'Are Ye Able?' Said The Master" (AG)
"Have Thine Own Way Lord" (AG)
"Here I Am, Lord" (UMH)
"I Surrender All" (AG)
"Jesus Calls Us" (AG)
"Jesus I Come" (WC)
"Let There Be Peace On Earth" (UMH)
"Lord, Speak To Me" (UMH)
"Make Me A Captive, Lord" (UMH)
"Open My Eyes, That I May See" (UMH)
"Take My Life And Let It Be" (AG)

FORGIVENESS / REDEMPTION

"O Love Divine, What Hast Thou Done" (WC)

GOALS/GUIDANCE

"All The Way My Savior Leads Me" (AG)
"Close To Thee" (UMH)
"Day By Day" (WC)
"He Leadth Me" (AG)
"O To Be Like Thee!" (AG)
"Savior, Like A Shepherd Lead Us" (AG)
"We Gather Together" (AG)

GRACE / MERCY

"He Lifted Me" (AG)
"Just As I Am" (AG)

HEALING / HELP

"Holy Ghost With Light Divine" (AG)
"How Sweet The Name Of Jesus Sounds" (AG)
"I Stand Amazed In The Presence" (UMH)
"Make Me A Blessing" (AG)
"Redeemed How I Love To Proclaim It" (AG)
"This Is A Day Of New Beginnings" (UMH)

HOPE

"My Hope Is Built" (UMH)

JOY

"For The Beauty Of The Earth" (AG)
"He Touched Me" (UMH)
"In The Garden" (AG)

LOVE

"Even Me" (AG)
"His Loving Kindness" (AG)
"In Heavenly Love Abiding" (AG)
"Love Divine, All Love Excelling" (AG)
"O Perfect Love" (AG)

PEACE / CALM

"I Need Thee Every Hour" (AG)

PRAISE / THANKS

"Breathe On Me, Breath Of God" (AG)
"Come, Ye Thankful People Come" (AG)
"Holy, Holy, Holy" (AG)
"How Great Thou Art" (AG)
"I Love To Tell The Story" (AG)
"Joyful, Joyful We Adore Thee" (AG)
"Now Thank We All Our God" (AG)
"O For A Thousand Tongues" (AG)
"To God Be The Glory" (AG)

PRAYER

"Lord, Speak To Me" (AG)
"Sweet Hour Of Prayer" (AG)

PROTECTION

"A Mighty Fortress" (AG)
"A Shelter In The Time Of Storm" (AG)
"O God, Our Help In Ages Past" (UMH)
"Rock Of Ages" (WC)

TRUST

"Be Still, My Soul" (AG)
"DO Lord Remember Me" (UMH)
"Gracious Spirit, Dwell With Me" (AG)
"Great Is Thy Faithfulness" (AG)
"O Thou, In Whose Presence" (UMH)
" Out Of The Depth I Cry To You" (WC)
"Tis So Sweet To Trust In Jesus" (UMH)
"Trust And Obey" (AG)

SELF-HELP BOOKS LIST and INTERNET WEBSITE LIST

Between counseling, I read piles of self-help books suggested by counselors and ministers or that I found in libraries and catalogs. I haven't read all of them cover to cover, some I only read specific topics. Some are more recent through classes at college or by way of webinars. Here is part of my healing library by topics.

ABUSE:

Bradshaw, John. "Healing The Shame That Binds You". Deerfield Beach, Florida: Health Communications, Inc. 1988.

Courtright, John and Sid Rogers. "What To Do When You Find Out . . . Your Wife Was Sexually Abused". Grand Rapids, Michigan: Zondervan Publishing House. 1994.

Engel,Beverly. "The Right To Innocence - Healing The Trauma Of Childhood Sexual Abuse". New York: Ivy Books. 1989.

Grubman-Black, Stephen D. "Broken Boys/ Mending Men - Recovery From Childhood Sexual Abuse". Bradenton, Florida: Human Services Institute. 1990.

Hill, Elsie I. "Abused But Chosen - The Unforgettable Life Story Of An Abused Child". Harrison, Arizona. 1983.

Hunter, Mic. "Abused Boys - The Neglected Victims Of Sexual Abuse". New York: Fawcett Columbine. 1990.

Maltz, Wendy and Beverly Holman. "Incest And Sexuality - A Guide To Understanding And Healing". Lexington, Massachusetts: Lexington Books. 1987.

Nakagawa, Donna Jackson. "Childhood Disrupted: How Your Biography Becomes Your Biology and How You Can Heal." New York: Atria Books. 2015.

Payne, Jennie S. RN, MSN, Sabrina Downs RN, MSN, and Karen Newman RN, MSN. "Helping The Abused Woman". Springhouse, PA:Nursing '86/ Springhouse Corp. September 1986.

Seamands, David A. "Healing Of Memories". Wheaton, Illinois: Victor Books/S P Publications, Inc. 1985.

Stadler, Matthew. "The Sex Offender". New York: Harper Perennial. 1994.

Wilson, Sandra D. "Released From Shame - Recovery From Adult Children Of Dysfunctional Families". Downers Grove, Illinois: People Helper Books/InterVarsity Press. 1990.

EMOTIONAL ISSUES:

Adams, Ramona S., Herbert A. Otto, and Audeane S. Cowely. "Letting Go: Uncomplicating Your Life". New York: MacMillan Publishing Co. Inc. 1980.

Allen, Marvin. "Angry Men, Passive Men - Understanding The Roots Of Men's Anger And How To Move Beyond It". New York: Fawcett Columbine. 1993.

Amen, Daniel G., M.D. "Change Your Brain Change Your Life". New York: Harmony Books.2015.
Braiker, Harriet, PhD. "Getting Up When You're Feeling Down". Lincoln, NE: iUniverse/Putnam. 1988. Also check out the guide published in 2001.

Brown, Brene, Ph.D., LMSW. "Daring Greatly". New York: Averly. 2012.

Crater, Les, Dr. and Dr. Frank Minirth. "The Anger Workbook - A 13 - Step Interactive Plan To Help You . . . ". Nashville, TN: Thomas Nelson Publishers. 1993.
Chandler, Anankha K. "Therapist In A Book - Emotional Healing". Granite Bay, CA: Penmarin Books. 2001.

Donnelly, Doris. "Learning To Forgive". Nashville, TN: Abingdon Press. 1979.

Freudenberger, Herbert J. "Burnout". 1985. This book is available on Amazon, but I could not find the name of the publisher.

Glende, Nancy H. "Forgiving Is The Only Real Solution To Violence". Cleveland, OH: Noelani Publishing Company, Inc. 1994.

Gopin, Marc, PhD. "Healing The Heart Of Conflict 8 Crucial Steps To Making Peace With Yourself And Others". Emmaus,PA: Rodale Press. 2004.

Gray, Jeffrey. "The Psychology Of Fear And Stress". New York: World University Library. 1972.

Handly, Robert. "Anxiety And Panic Attacks - Their Cause And Cure". New York: Fawcett Crest. 1985.

Lerner, Harriet, PhD. "The Dance Of Anger - A Woman's Guide To Changing The Patterns Of Intimate Relationships". New York: William Morrow/ HarperCollins Publishers. 2014.

Marmorstein, Jerome and Nanette Marmorstein. "Awakening From Depression - A Mind/ Body Approach To Emotional Recovery". Santa Barbara, CA: Woodbridge Press. 1992.

Pearsoll, Paul,PhD. "Super Immunity - Master Your Emotions And Improve Your Health". New York: McGraw-Hill Book Company. 1987.

Reale, Joan RN, MSN. "Life Changes Can They Cause Disease?". Springhouse, PA: Nursing '87/ Springhouse Corp. July 1987.

Seamands, David A. "Healing for Damaged Emotions". Wheaton, Illinois: Victor Books. 1981.

Selye, Hans,MD. "Stress Without Distress". New York: Signet Book. 1974.

Sharpe, Robert, Dr. "Self-Help For Your Anxiety - The Proven 'Anxiety Antidote' Method". New York: Barnes and Noble Books. 1990.

Williams, Redford, MD and Virginia Williams,PhD. "Anger Kills - Seventeen Strategies For Controlling The Hostility That Can Harm Your Health". New York: Harper Perennial. 1994.

RELATIONSHIP ISSUES:

Beattie, Melody. "Beyond Codependency and Getting Better All the Time". New York: Hazelden Book/ HarperCollins Publishers. 1989.

Beattie, Melody. "Codependent No More". Center City, Minnesota: Hazelden Books. 1992.

Bloomfield, Harold H., MD. "Making Peace With Your Parents - The Key To Enriching Your Life And All Your Relationships". New York: Ballantine Books. 1983.

Clarke, Jean I. "Self-Esteem: A Family Affair". San Francisco, CA:Harper. 1978.

Evans, Patricia. "The Verbally Abusive Relationship". Holbrook, Massachusetts: Adams Publishing. 1995.

Fisher, Bruce,Dr. "Rebuilding When Your Relationship Ends". San Luis Obispo, CA. 1995.

Kiley, Dan, Dr. "Living Together Feeling Alone: Healing Your Hidden Loneliness". New York: Prentice Hall Press. 1989.

Levy, Barrie. "In Love And In Danger - A Teen's Guide To Breaking Free Of Abusive Relationships". Seattle, WA: Seal Press. 1993.

Jones, Ann and Susan Schecter. "When Love Goes Wrong - What To Do When You Can't Do Anything Right - Strategies For Women With Controlling Partners". New York: HarperCollins Publishers. 1992.

Nelson, Bradley, Dr. "The Emotional Code". Mesquite, Nevada: Wellness Unmasked Publishing. 2007.

NorWood, Robin. "Women Who Love Too Much – When You Keep Wishing and Hoping He'll Change". New York: Pocket Books/Simon and Schuster, Inc. 1985.

Sande, Ken. "The Peacemaker – A Biblical Guide To Resolving Personal Conflict". Grand Rapids, Michigan: Baker Book House. 1991.

Schlessinger, Laura, DR. "Ten Stupid Things Women Do To Mess Up Their Lives". New York: Harper Perennial. 1995.

Van Kaam, Adrain and Susan Muto. "The Power of Appreciation – A New Approach To Personal and Relational Healing". New York: Crossroad. 1993.

White, John. "Parents in Pain – A Book of Comfort and Counsel". Downers Grove, Illinois: InterVarsity Press. 1979.

Whiteman, Thomas A.,PhD and Randy Petersen. "Love Gone Wrong - What To Do Where You Are Attracted To The Wrong Person Over And Over". Nashville, TN: Thomas Nelson Publishers. 1994.

TREATMENT:

Batie, Howard F. "Healing Body, Mind, And Spirit - A Guide To Energy-Based Healing". St. Paul, Minnesota: Llewellyn Worldwide. 2003.

Corey, Gerald. "Theory And Practice Of Counseling And Psychotherapy". Monterey,CA: Brooks/Cole Publishing Company. 1977.

DeWet, Pieter, MD. "Heal Thyself - Transform Your Life - Transform Your Health". Mustang,OK: Tate Publishing and Enterprise, LLC. 2010.

Hay, Louise L. "Heal Your Body". New York: Hay House, Inc. 1984. Also check out - "You Can Heal Your Life".

Hoff, Lee Ann. "People In Crisis - Understanding And Helping". San Francisco, CA: Jossey-Bass Publishers. 1995.

Klein, Donald F.,MD and Paul H. Wender, MD. "Understanding Depression - A Complete Guide To Its Diagnosis And Treatment". New York: Oxford University Press. 1993.

Lake, James H.,MD and David Spiegel, MD. "Complementary And Alternative Treatments: In Mental Health Care". Washington D.C.: American Psychiatric Publishing, Inc. 2007.

Lake, James,MD. "Integrative Mental Health Care: A Therapist's Handbook". New York: Norton Professional Books/ W.W. Norton and Company. 2009.

Lawless, Julia. "The Complete Illustrated Guide To Aromatherapy". Rockport, Massachusetts: Element. 1997.

Lawless, Julia. "The Encyclopedia Of Essential Oils". San Francisco, CA: Conari Press. 2013.

Marich, Jamie, PhD. "EMDR Made Simple: 4 Approaches to Using EMDR with Every Client". Eau Claire,WI: Premier Publishing & Media. 2011.

Porges, Stephen W. "The Pocket Guide to the Polyvagal Theory". New York: W.W. Norton & Company. 2017.
Rosenberg, Stanley. "Acessing the Healing Power of the Vagus Nerve". Berkeley,CA: North Altantic Books. 2017.
Shapiro, Francine,PhD. "Eye Movement Desensitization And Reprocessing - Basic Principles, Protocols, And Procedures". New York/ The Guilford Press. 2001.

Watson, Brenda,C.N.C. "The Detox strategy - Vibrant Health In 5 Easy Steps. New York: Free Press/ Simon and Schuster, Inc. 2008.

Worwood, Valerie Ann. "The Complete Book Of Essential Oils And Aromatherapy". Novato, CA: New World Library. 1991.

RELIGIOUS APPROACHES:

Dossey, Larry, MD. "Healing Words - The Power Of Prayer And Practice Of Medicine". San Francisco, CA: Harper San Francisco/ A Division Of HarperCollins Publisher. 1993.

Dyer, Wayne W. "Real Magic Creating Miracles In Everyday Life". New York: HarperCollins Publishers. 1991.

Elliot, Elisabeth. "Passion And Purity". Old Tappan, New Jersey: Power Books/ Fleming H. Revell. 1984.

Foster, Richard. "Prayer Treasury". New York: HarperCollins Publishers, Inc. 1994.
Fowler, James W. "Stages Of Faith - The Psychology Of Human Development And The Quest For Meaning". San Francisco: Harper. 1981.

Linn, Matthew, Sheila Fabricant, and Dennis Linn. "Healing The Eight Stages Of Life". New York: Paulist Press. 1988. Also check out other Paulist Press Books: "Healing Life Hurts", "Healing Of Memories", "Healing The Greatest Hurt", " Prayer Course For Healing Life's Hurts", and "Prayer With Another For Healing".

Lockyer, Herbert. "All The Promises Of The Bible". Grand Rapids, Michigan: Zondervan. 1962.

Schaeffer, Edith. "Affliction - A Compassionate Christian Look At Understanding The Reality Of Pain And Suffering In Our Lives". Old Tappan, New Jersey: Fleming H. Revell Company. 1973.

Seuss, Dr. "Oh, The Places You'll Go!". New York: Random House. 1990.

Wagner, James K. "Blessed To Be A Blessing". Nashville,TN/: The Upper Room. 1980. Especially look at Chapter 6 - "Forgiveness Is Key to Good Health" and Appendix B - Resources for Healing Prayer and Meditation.

SURVIVAL:

Angelou, Maya. "I Know Why the Caged Bird Sings" New York: Random House. 2015.

Fahy, Mary. "The Tree That Survived The Winter". New York: Paulist Press. 1989.

ADDICTION TREATMENT:

Arenson, Gloria. "A Substance Called Food How To Understand, Control And Recover From Addictive Eating". Blue Ridge Summit, PA: Tab Books. 1989.

Atkins, Robert C. "The New Diet Revolution". New York: HarperCollins Publishers. 2009.

Urschel III, Harold C.,MD. "Healing The Addicted Brain - The Revolutionary Science-Based, Alcoholism And Addiction Recovery Program". Naperville, Illinois: Sourcebooks, Inc. 2009.

Introduction to Internet Resources

This resource list was complied from https://metoomvmt.org/resources and from goggle searches. The Me Too site is very helpful. This by no means all the resources available on the internet. You can hone in on the specific issue(s) that you need to research or expand on.

GENERAL RESOURCES

- Adult Children of Alcoholics
  1-310-534-1815
  <information@ACAWSO.com>
- Alliance of Information and Referral Service
  www.airs.org
- American Counseling Association
  www.counseling.org
- Dana Foundation – supporting neuroscience and brain research
  www.dana.org
- Day One – dating abuse
  1-800-214-4150
  https://www.dayoneny.org
- Gamblers Anonymous National Services
  <gamblersanonymous.org>
- Girls for Gender Equity-sexual harassment
  https://www.ggenyc.org/publications/
- Narcotic Anonymous
  www.na.org

- National Online Resource Center on Violence Against Women
  Phone: 1-800-537-2238   fax: 1-717-545-9456
  https://vawnet.org
- National Street Harassment Hotline
  1-855-897-5910
  www.stopstreetharassment.org/our-work/nationalhotline/
- Overeaters Anonymous
  www.oa.org
- Sexaholics Anonymous
  www.sa.org
- Substance Abuse and Mental Health Services Administration
  <samnsa.gov>

LEGAL RESOURCES

- ACLU
- 1-888-428-7581

- It Happened to Alexa Foundation
- 1-877-77A-LEXA
- www.ithappenedtoalexa.org
- Legal Aid for Survivors of Sexual Assault (LASSA)
- 1-800-991-5153
- www.legalaidforsurvivors.org/contact/
- MACASA's Sexual Assault Legal Institute (SALI)
- 1-301-565-2277
- https://www.macasa.org/survivors/sali
- National Women's Law Center

- 1-202-319-3053
- https://nwlc.org
- Surv Justice
- 1-202-869-0699
- www.survjustice.org
- Rape, Abuse, Incest National Network (RAINN)
- State database: 1-800-656-4673
- https://www.appsrainn.org/policy/
- Women's Law Organization
- 1-800-799-7233
- https://www.womenslaw.org

MEDICAL and PHYSICAL RESOURCES

- American college of Obstetricians and Gynecologist
- <www.acog.org
- Healthcare Center Directory
- 1-877-464-4772
- https://findahealthcarecenter.hrsa.gov
- International Association of Forensic Nurses
- Phone: 1-410-626-7805   Fax: 1-410-626-7804
- www.forensicnurses.org/defaullt.aspex
- Sexual Assault Nurse Examiner (SANE)
- www.sane-sart.com
- Start Your Recovery – drugs, alcohol, physical, and emotional
- https://startyourrecovery.org
- The Center for Disease Control National Prevention Information Network – HIV/AIDS and more
- 1-800-458-5231
- https://npin.cdc.gov

DOMESTIC PARTNER VIOLENCE RESOURCES

- American Overseas Domestic Violence Crisis Center
- 1-503-203-1444
- https://pathwaystosafety.org
- National Domestic Violence Hotline
- 1-800-799-SAFE
- www.thehotline.org
- National Teen Dating Abuse Online Helpline
- www.loveisrespect.org
- Safe Horizon
- 1-800=621-4673
- https://www.safehorizon.org/get-help/domestic-violence/#our-program/
- The National Council of Juvenile and Family Court Judges (NCJFCJ)
- 1-775-507-4777
- www.ncjfcj.org

RESOURCES FOR SURVIVORS OF CHILD ABUSE AND PREVENTION

- Adult Survivors of Child Abuse
- <www.ascasupport.org>
- Cyber Tipline
- 1-800-843-5678
- www.cybertipline.com
- Child Molestation Prevention (CMRPI)
- <childmolestationprevent.org>
- Darkness to Light – prevent abuse

- 1-866-367-5444
- www.d2l.org
- Justice for Children's Alliance
- 1-202-548-0090
- www.nationalchildrensalliance.org
- Me Too Movement
- https://metoomvmt.org/resources
- Missing and Exploited Children
- 1-800-THE-LOST
- <CyberTipline.org> and www.missingkids.org
- Psychology Today – articles and counselor location in your area and style of therapy
- www.psychologytoday.com
- Stop It Now
- 1-888-PREVENT
- <www.stopitnow
- <survivor manual.com>
- Incest Survivors Anonymous
- <siawso.org>

RESOURCES FOR PARTNERS OF SURVIVORS OF ABUSE

- <supportforpartners.org>
- Partners of Adults Sexual Abuse as Children
- <pasac.net>

RESOURCES FOR MALE SURVIVORS

- 1 in 6
- https://1in6.org
- Dr. Jim Hopper PhD
- https://www.jimhopper.com
- <malesurvive.org>
- The Association of Alberta Sexual Assault Services
- 1-403-237-6905
- https://aasas.ca/support-and-information/men-and-sexual-assault/
- Together We Heal
- 1-754-234-7975
- <together-we-heal.org/therapts.btml>

RESOURCES FOR PEOPLE OF COLOR

- Asian Pacific Institute on Gender Based Violence (APIGBV)
- 1-415-568-3315
- https://www.api-gbv.gov
- Black Women's Blueprint (BWB)
- 1-347-533-9102
- <blackwomensblueprint.org>
- Casa de Esperanza
- 1-651-772-1611
- https://casadesperanza.org
- Incite!
- www.incite-national.org/page/dangerous-intersections

- Mending the Sacred Hoop
- 1-844-7NATIVE and 1-888-305-1650
- https://mshoop.org/resources
- National Indigenous Women's Resource Center
- 1-406-477-3896
- www.niwrc.org
- The National Organization of Sisters of Color Ending Sexual Assault (SCESA)
- <sisterslead.org/resources/all-local-communities-of-color-sexual-assault-oranizations/>
- The Women Lawyers Division of the National Bar Association
- 1-884-345-2221
- https://www..nbawld.org

RESOURCES FOR LGBTQ SURVIVORS

- Association for Lesbian, Gay, Bisexual, and Transgender Issues
- www.algbtic.org/therapist-resource-listing.html
- FORGE – For Ourselves: Reworking Gender Expression
- 1-414-559-2123
- <forge-forward.org>
- National Coalition of Anti-Violence Programs
- 1-212-714-1141
- https://avp.org/neavp/
- The National Center for Transgender Equality (NCTE)
- 1-202-642-4542

- https://transequality.org/know-your-rights/survivors-violence
- The Network La Red
- 1-617-742-4911
- <tnir.org/en/>
- The NW Network
- 1-206-568-1777
- https://www.nwnetwork.org
- The Trevor Project
- 1-866-488-7386
- https://www.thetrevorproject.org/#sm.0000008y4x8 ruid6jwje7h50o4px7

RESOURCES FOR SURVIVORS WITH DISABILITIES

- Deaf Abused Women's Network (DAWN)
- 1-202-559-5366
- <deafdawn.org>
- National Disabilities Rights Network
- !-202-408-9514
- www.napsa-now.org/get-help-in-your-area/
- Women's Health.gov
- 1-800-994-9662
- https://www.womenshealth.gov/relationships-and-safety/other-types/violence-against-women-disabilities

RESOURCES FOR UNDOCUMENTED INDIVIDUALS

- \<domesticshelters.org\>
- Latino Immigrants (MALDEF)
- www.maldef.org/about/index.html
- U.S. Citizenship and Immigration Services
- https://www.uscis.gov/news/fact-sheets/information-legal-rights-available-immigrant-victims-domestic-violence-united-states-and-facts-about-immigranting. . .

RESOURCES FOR SEXUAL ASSAULT IN THE WORKPLACE

- Equal Employment Opportunity Commission (EEOC)
- https://www.eeoc.gov
- Equal Rights Advocates
- 1-415-621-0505
- https://www.equalrights.org
- The United States Department of Labor, Women's Bureau
- https://www.dol.gov/wb/info_.about_wb/regions/regional_offices.htm
- Times Up Legal Defense Fund
- https://www.timesupnow.com

RESOURCES FOR COLLEGE STUDENTS

- End Rape On Campus (EROC)
- 1-424-777-3762
- <endrapeoncampus.org>
- Not Alone.gov
- https://www.justice.gov/OVW/protecting-students-sexual-assault Title IV from DOJ
- The American Association of University Women (AAUW)
- 1-202-785-7700
- https://www.aauw.org/resource/campus-sexual-assault-tool-kit/

RESOURCES FOR MILITARY SURVIVORS

- Mason Veterans and Servicemembers Legal Clinic
- 1-703-993-8214
- https://safehelpline.org
- Stateside Legal
- 1-855-828-6636
- <statesidelegal.org/military-sexual-trauma-resources-women>
- The U.S. Department of Veterans Affairs
- 1-844-698-6636
- https://www.va.gov
- United States Naval Academy's Legal Counsel Program
- 1-410-293-9000
- https://www,usa.edu/SAPRO/resources.php

HUMAN TRAFFICKING RESOURCES

- Department of Homeland Security
- https://www.dhs.goy/state-and-local-anti-human-trafficking-resources
- National Human Trafficking Resource Center
- 1-888-373-7888
- https://humantraffickinghotline.org   Text: 233733
- Polaris
- 1-202-790-6300
- https://polarisproject.org/resources
- Shared Hope International
- 1-866-HER-LIFE
- https://sharedhope.org/what-we-do/restore/
- U.S. Department of Justice Trafficking in Persons and Worker Exploitation Complaint (FBI)
- 1-888-428-7581
- The CyberTipline
- www.scag.gov
- Missing and Exploited Children
- 1-800-THE-LOST
- www.missingkids.org   and   <CyberTipline.org>

RESOURCES FOR INCARCERATED SEXUAL ABUSE VICTIM

- Just Detention International (JDI)
- East Coast – Phone: 1-202-506-3333   Fax: 1-202-506-7971

- Headquarters – Phone: 1-213-384-1400   Fax: 1-213-384-1411
- info@justdetention.org   https://justdetention.org/what-we-do/helping-prisoner-rape-survivors/
- Just Now
- 1-510-838-7654
- https://www.justicenow.org
- Washington Coalition of Sexual Assault Programs (WCSAP)
- Phone: 1-360-754-7584   Fax: 1-360-786-8707   ITTY: 1-360-709-0305

RESOURCES FOR SUICIDE PREVENTION AND SUICIDE ATTEMPT SURVIVORS

- Adverse Childhood Experiences (ACEs)
- <http://ACEsTooHigh.com
- Centers for Disease Control and Prevention (CDC)
- !-800-232-4636
- http://www.cdc.gov/ace/outcomes.htm
- Health.com – resource for many related issues
- http://www,health.comdepression>
- Live Through This
- Text: HOME to 741741
- https://livethroughthis.org   <warmline.org>
- Psychology Today – find a counselor in your locale and articles
- https://www.psychologytoday.com/blog
- National Alliance on Mental Illness (NAMI)
- Prevention hotline: 1-855-879-5439

- https://www.nami.org/persona-stories
- Substance Abuse and Mental Health Services Administration (SAMHSA)
- Suicide prevention: 1-800-273-TALK   National Hotline: 1-800-662-HELP
- https://store.samhsa.gov/product/Stories-Of-Hope-And-Recovery-A-Video-Guide
- Suicide Awareness Voices of Education
- Prevention hotline: 1-800-273-TALK
- https://save.org/findhelp/attempt-survivor-resources
- Suicide info – The Centre for Suicide Prevention (CSP) Canada
- 1-833-456-4566 (4357)   Text: 45645
- https://www.suicideinf.ca/resources/suicideattemptsurvivors
- Suicide Prevention Lifeline
- 1-800-273-8255
- <htps://suicidepreventionlifeline.org>

SHARE YOUR STORY

- The Clothesline Project
- <clotheslineproject.info>
- When You're Ready
- <WhenYoureReady.org/share/>